Ceviche Recipes

A Ceviche Cookbook with Delicious Ceviche Recipes

By
BookSumo Press
All rights reserved

Published by
http://www.booksumo.com

LEGAL NOTES

All Rights Reserved. No Part Of This Book May Be Reproduced Or Transmitted In Any Form Or By Any Means. Photocopying, Posting Online, And / Or Digital Copying Is Strictly Prohibited Unless Written Permission Is Granted By The Book's Publishing Company. Limited Use Of The Book's Text Is Permitted For Use In Reviews Written For The Public.

Table of Contents

Full Barcelona Ceviche 7
Simple Ceviche Formulae 8
Ferdinand's Favorite 9
Hot Hawaiian Ceviche 10
Imitation Ceviche 11
Arizona Shrimp Ceviche 12
Southern Sole Ceviche 13
Spiced Kale Ceviche 14
Ceviche Cups 15
Boardwalk Ceviche 16
Wednesday's Lunch Ceviche 17
Louisiana Ceviche 18
Catalina's Cabbage Ceviche 19
West Indian Ceviche 20
Bahamian Ceviche 21
New England Ceviche Bowls 22
Sunday's Ceviche 23
Isabelle's Ceviche 24
Indonesian Ceviche 25
Hot Cilantro Ceviche 26
Pickled Papaya Ceviche 27
Ceviche Micronesia 28
Chicago Ceviche 29
Tangy Mustard Ceviche 30
Bonnie's Favorite Ceviche 31
Ceviche Brasileiro 32
Country Ceviche 33
Oriental Ceviche 34
Mango Ceviche Wraps 35
Naked Ceviche 36
Chipotle Ceviche 37

Ceviche in Tortilla Bowls 38
Ceviche Wraps II 39
Southwest Ceviche 40
Bethany Beach Ceviche 41
Greek Ceviche 42
Vegetarian Dream Ceviche 43
Hassan's Harbor Ceviche 44
Hot Ginger Ceviche 45
Fairbanks French Ceviche 46
Crunchy Crab Ceviche 47
Pineapple Ceviche with Fried Cinnamon Pastry 48
Pink Serrano Ceviche 49
Kissimmee Key Lime Ceviche 50
Ceviche Tilapia 51
Ceviche Bowls 52
Ceviche Gonzalez 53
Garden Ceviche 54
Big World Ceviche 55
New York Vegan Ceviche 56
Easy Vegetarian Ceviche 57
Hot Ceviche with Crab 58
Ceviche Mexicana 59
Portuguese Ceviche 60
Orange Ceviche 61
Weekend Ceviche 62
Sao Paulo Ceviche Toppers 63
Mango Salsa Ceviche 64
Michelle's Citrus Ceviche 65
Corn and Radish Ceviche Salad 66
Cynthia's Yam Ceviche 67
Ceviche Medellin 68
Ceviche with Spiced Bass 69
Hawaiian Meridian Ceviche 70

15-Minute Canned Ceviche 71
Peruvian Lunch Box Wraps 72
Ceviche Casablanca 73
"Deviled" Mushrooms 74
Weeknight Ceviche 75
Ceviche with Prawns 76
New England Ceviche with Plantains 77
Ceviche with Trout 78
Ceviche Jamaican 79
Ceviche Kabobs 80
Ceviche Autumn 81
Kiara's Mint Ginger Ceviche 82
6-Ingredient Ceviche 83
American Ceviche 84
Florida Summer Ceviche 85
Hot Central American Ceviche 86
Ceviche Siestas 87
My First Ceviche 88
10-Minute Tortilla Ceviche 89
Ceviche Scoops 90
Ceviche Guyana 91
How to Make a Ceviche 92
Ceviche Polynesia 93
Alaskan Ceviche 94
Tacos Argentina 95
Maria's Ceviche Platter 96
Pacific Island Ceviche 97
Hot Plum Tomato Ceviche 98
California Ceviche Boats 99

Full Barcelona Ceviche

🥣 Prep Time: 10 mins
🕐 Total Time: 4 hr 10 mins

Servings per Recipe: 8
Calories   122.7
Fat   2.8g
Cholesterol   130.6mg
Sodium   340.1mg
Carbohydrates   8.7g
Protein   16.1g

Ingredients

- 1/2 lb. shrimp, peeled and deveined
- 1/2 lb. squid, cleaned and sliced into rings
- 1/2 lb. scallops, quartered if large
- 1 (10 oz.) cans Rotel Tomatoes, drained
- 2 medium ripe tomatoes, seeded and diced
- 1/2 large cucumber, peeled and diced
- 1/2 large green pepper, diced
- 1/2 medium red sweet onion, diced
- 1/2 C. chopped fresh cilantro
- 1 tsp minced garlic
- 3/4 C. lime juice
- 1/2 tsp cumin
- 1 tbsp capers, chopped
- 1/2 C. hot and spicy hot V8
- 1 tbsp extra virgin olive oil
- 1 tsp Accent seasoning
- salt & pepper

Directions

1. Place a large saucepan of salted water over high heat. Bring it to a boil.
2. Cook in it the shrimp for 1 min. Drain it and place it in a bowl of ice-cold water.
3. Drain it and chop it. Place it aside.
4. Cook the squid in the same saucepan for 10 sec. Drain it, stir it into the cold water and drain it again.
5. Repeat the process with scallops cooking them for 60 sec.
6. Get a mixing bowl: Stir in it the scallops with shrimp, squid, and lime juice.
7. Cover the bowl and place it in the fridge for 60 min.
8. Once the time is up, stir the remaining ingredients into the seafood bowl. Toss them to coat.
9. Chill it in the fridge for 4 h then serve it.
10. Enjoy.

SIMPLE
Ceviche Formulae

Prep Time: 20 mins
Total Time: 20 mins

Servings per Recipe: 6
Calories 335.5
Fat 11.2g
Cholesterol 95.5mg
Sodium 859.0mg
Carbohydrates 0.8g
Protein 53.8g

Ingredients
3 lbs. boneless white fish, skinless, cubed
lime juice
orange juice
2 tbsp white vinegar
kosher salt & ground black pepper
2 tbsp olive oil
1/4 small red onion, chopped
3 green onions, trimmed and chopped
1 celery rib, chopped
2 tbsp cilantro, chopped

Directions
1. Get a mixing bowl: Stir in it the fish with the juice of 2 limes.
2. Chill it in the fridge for 16 min.
3. Get a mixing bowl: Whisk in it the juice of 1 lime, orange juice, vinegar, salt, pepper, and olive oil.
4. Drain the fish and add it with onion, green onion, celery, and cilantro. Toss them to coat.
5. Chill the ceviche in the fridge for 3 h then serve it.
6. Enjoy.

Ferdinand's Favorite

🥣 Prep Time: 2 hr 15 mins
🕐 Total Time: 2 hr 15 mins

Servings per Recipe: 24
Calories   29.8
Fat   2.2g
Cholesterol   1.2mg
Sodium   39.5mg
Carbohydrates   2.5g
Protein   0.2g

Ingredients

- 2 C. white fish fillets
- 1/2 C. lime juice, strained
- 1 C. carrot, cooked and cut into strips
- 1 C. tomatoes, peeled and chopped
- 1/2 C. green onion, chopped
- 1/3 C. cilantro, chopped
- 1 tbsp olive oil
- 2 tbsp white vinegar
- salt
- pepper
- 1/4 C. water
- 1/2 C. mayonnaise
- corn chips
- chopped lettuce

Directions

1. Get a mixing bowl: Stir in it the lime juice with fish. Cover it and place it in the fridge for 60 min.
2. Once the time is up, drain it and transfer it to a mixing bowl.
3. Add to it the carrots, tomatoes, onions, cilantro, oil, and vinegar.
4. Season them with a pinch of salt and pepper. Toss them to coat.
5. Use a plastic wrap to cover the bowl and chill it in the fridge for 60 min.
6. Once the time is up, stir in the mayo then serve your ceviche right away.
7. Enjoy.

HOT
Hawaiian Ceviche

🥣 Prep Time: 30 mins
🕒 Total Time: 45 mins

Servings per Recipe: 4
Calories 171.6
Fat 15.4g
Cholesterol 0.0mg
Sodium 37.1mg
Carbohydrates 9.4g
Protein 2.4g

Ingredients
10 oz. coconut milk
2 tbsp chopped ginger
2 tbsp grated horseradish
3 jalapeno peppers, seeded and minced
3 tbsp chopped cilantro
1 lime, juice
12 oz. sashimi-grade tuna, cubed
1 tomatoes, seeded and diced
1 small red onion, julienned
1 scallion, julienned

Directions
1. Place a large saucepan over medium heat. Stir in it the coconut milk, ginger, and horseradish.
2. Bring them to a rolling boil. Let them cook until they reduce by 1/4.
3. Once the time is up, strain the milk sauce and discard the solids.
4. Get a mixing bowl: Stir in it the tuna, tomato, jalapeno, cilantro, lime juice and coconut sauce.
5. Adjust the seasoning of your ceviche then places it in the fridge until ready to serve.
6. Enjoy.

Imitation Ceviche

Prep Time: 10 mins
Total Time: 10 mins

Servings per Recipe: 4
Calories	110.3
Fat	1.2g
Cholesterol	16.9mg
Sodium	1587.3mg
Carbohydrates	14.4g
Protein	11.3g

Ingredients

- 2 C. white fish fillets
- 1/2 C. lime juice, strained
- 1 C. carrot, cooked and cut into strips
- 1 C. tomatoes, peeled and chopped
- 1/2 C. green onion, chopped
- 1/3 C. cilantro, chopped
- 1 tbsp olive oil
- 2 tbsp white vinegar
- salt
- pepper
- 1/4 C. water
- 1/2 C. mayonnaise
- corn chips
- chopped lettuce

Directions

1. Get a mixing bowl: Stir in it all the ingredients.
2. Place it in the fridge and let it chill for at least 2 h.
3. Serve your ceviche with some chips or tostadas.
4. Enjoy.

ARIZONA
Shrimp Ceviche

🥣 Prep Time: 45 mins
🕒 Total Time: 50 mins

Servings per Recipe: 6
Calories 335.0
Fat 8.5g
Cholesterol 345.6mg
Sodium 641.3mg
Carbohydrates 17.8g
Protein 46.9g

Ingredients
3 lbs. small shrimp
1 bunch coriander
2 red onions, sliced
1 jalapeno pepper, chopped
10 lemons, juice
2 tbsp olive oil
4 tbsp tomato sauce
1/2 C. Worcestershire sauce
1 pinch salt

Directions
1. Place a heavy saucepan over medium heat. Stir in it the water with Worcestershire sauce and salt.
2. Bring them to a boil. Stir in the shrimp and cook it for 3 min. Drain it and chop it.
3. Get a mixing bowl: Stir in it the shrimp with coriander, onions, lemon juice, jalapeno pepper to taste, tomato sauce and olive oil.
4. Adjust the seasoning of your ceviche then chill it in the fridge for 10 min. Serve it with some crackers.
5. Enjoy.

Southern Sole Ceviche

Prep Time: 30 mins
Total Time: 24 hr 30 mins

Servings per Recipe: 6
Calories   403.0
Fat   37.6g
Cholesterol   34.0mg
Sodium   350.5mg
Carbohydrates   7.9g
Protein   10.2g

Ingredients

- 1 lb. sole fillet, cubed
- 1 C. salad oil
- 1/4 C. chopped cilantro
- 1 C. sliced pimento-stuffed green olives
- 2 C. minced onions
- 2/3 C. lime juice
- 2 garlic cloves, minced
- 2 bay leaves
- 2 - 3 pickled jalapeno peppers, minced
- salt and pepper
- lettuce and sliced celery

Directions

1. Get a mixing bowl: Stir in it all the ingredients.
2. Layover it a plastic wrap to cover it. Chill it in the fridge for 14 to 24 h.
3. Once the time is up, discard the bay leaves. Serve your ceviche with some lettuce.
4. Enjoy.

SPICED
Kale Ceviche

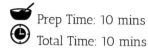
Prep Time: 10 mins
Total Time: 10 mins

Servings per Recipe: 6
Calories 117.8
Fat 6.3g
Cholesterol 0.0mg
Sodium 121.6mg
Carbohydrates 15.7g
Protein 2.6g

Ingredients
1 bunch kale, leaves
1 large avocado, peeled
1 tbsp lemon juice
1/4 tsp salt
1/2 tsp crushed red pepper flakes
1/2 red bell pepper
1 small carrot, grated
1/2 purple onion, chopped
1 1/2 C. mandarin orange segments

Directions
1. Get a mixing bowl: Toss in it the kale with avocado, lemon juice, salt and red pepper flakes.
2. Mix them well with your hands until they avocado become mashed and smooth.
3. Add the rest of the ingredients. Toss them to coat.
4. Chill your ceviche in the fridge for 35 min then serve it.
5. Enjoy.

Ceviche Cups

🥣 Prep Time: 10 mins
🕐 Total Time: 10 mins

Servings per Recipe: 4
Calories   278.8
Fat   15.1g
Cholesterol   37.4mg
Sodium   346.6mg
Carbohydrates   15.1g
Protein   23.6g

Ingredients

- 2 (6 oz.) cans albacore tuna in water, drained
- 1/2 C. sweet onion, diced
- 1 large tomatoes, seeded and diced
- 1 small cucumber, peeled and diced
- 1/4 C. cilantro,
- 1 - 2 serrano chili, diced
- 2 - 3 limes, juice
- 1 tbsp olive oil
- salt
- pepper
- 1 large avocado, diced
- 8 tostadas

Directions

1. Get a mixing bowl: Stir in it the tuna, onion, tomato, cucumber, and cilantro.
2. Pour over them the lime juice, olive oil, salt, and pepper. Toss them to coat.
3. Stir in the serrano chilies, followed by avocado.
4. Spoon your ceviche into tostadas then serve them right away.
5. Enjoy.

BOARDWALK
Ceviche

Prep Time: 20 mins
Total Time: 2 hr 20 mins

Servings per Recipe: 20
Calories 171.7
Fat 2.0g
Cholesterol 68.6mg
Sodium 1177.8mg
Carbohydrates 11.7g
Protein 26.8g

Ingredients

5 tomatoes, peeled and diced
1 onion, Red, diced
6 lb. halibut, cubed
32 oz. lime juice
2 C. Clamato juice
2/3 C. ketchup
2 oz. sugar
1.5 oz. salt
1 English cucumber, seeded and cubed
1 bunch cilantro

Directions

1. Get a mixing bowl: Stir in it the cucumber, onion, tomato, and halibut.
2. Add the lime juice with clamato juice and ketchup. Toss them to coat.
3. Cover the bowl with a plastic wrap and refrigerate it for 2 h.
4. Once the time is up, serve your ceviche with some chips.
5. Enjoy.

Wednesday's Lunch Ceviche

Prep Time: 15 mins
Total Time: 15 mins

Servings per Recipe: 4
Calories   689.3
Fat   28.5g
Cholesterol   32.3mg
Sodium   92.8mg
Carbohydrates   89.0g
Protein   22.9g

Ingredients

- 3/4 lb. tuna, filets
- 2 tomatoes, diced
- 1 green pepper, seeded and diced
- 1 - 3 hot red chili pepper, diced
- 1/2 C. cucumber, peeled, seeded and diced
- 1 C. lime juice
- 2 C. coconut milk
- salt & pepper

Directions

1. Get a mixing bowl: Stir in it all the ingredients.
2. Cover the bowl and chill it in the fridge for at least 2 h.
3. Once the time is up, adjust the seasoning of your ceviche then serve it.
4. Enjoy.

LOUISIANA
Ceviche

🥣 Prep Time: 1 hr
🕒 Total Time: 5 hr

Servings per Recipe: 6
Calories   207.6
Fat   14.0g
Cholesterol   41.5mg
Sodium   467.1mg
Carbohydrates   9.3g
Protein   12.8g

Ingredients

- 1 lb. catfish fillet, cut into pieces
- 1 tsp grated lemon zest
- 1/2 C. lemon juice
- 1 tsp grated lime zest
- 1/2 C. lime juice
- 2 tbsp extra-virgin olive oil
- 1 C. seeded diced ripe tomatoes
- 1/2 C. diced red onion
- 2 garlic cloves, sliced
- 2 tbsp cilantro leaves
- 1 tbsp oregano leaves
- 1 jalapeno pepper, seeded, deveined, and minced
- 1 tsp salt
- 1/2 tsp sugar
- 1 avocado, pitted, peeled, and diced

Directions

1. Get a Ziploc bag; stir in it the fish with lemon and lime zest and juices.
2. Seal the bag and shake it to coat. Place it in the fridge for 5 h to 18 h.
3. Once the time is up, drain the fish and transfer it to a mixing bowl.
4. Add to it the rest of the ingredients and toss them to coat. Serve it with some crackers.
5. Enjoy.

Catalina's Cabbage Ceviche

Prep Time: 30 mins
Total Time: 31 mins

Servings per Recipe: 12
Calories	108.7
Fat	1.0g
Cholesterol	79.6mg
Sodium	378.1mg
Carbohydrates	15.8g
Protein	11.3g

Ingredients

- 1 head green cabbage, shredded
- 6 small English cucumbers, shredded
- 1 large onion,
- 1 yellow pepper, shredded
- 4 large garlic cloves, crushed and mashed with 1 tsp. salt
- 4 tomatoes, seeded and chopped
- 4 large limes, juice
- 1 C. cilantro,
- salt and pepper
- 1 lb. shrimp, peeled and deveined

Directions

1. Bring a large saucepan of water to a boil. Cook in it the shrimp for 2 min.
2. Drain it and chop it.
3. Get a baking dish: Stir in it all the ingredients including the chopped shrimp.
4. cover the bowl and place it in the fridge for 30 min. Serve it with some chips.
5. Enjoy.

WEST INDIAN
Ceviche

Prep Time: 40 mins
Total Time: 42 mins

Servings per Recipe: 4
Calories 470.4
Fat 13.0g
Cholesterol 265.0mg
Sodium 1131.5mg
Carbohydrates 61.3g
Protein 42.5g

Ingredients
1/2 lb. salmon, cubed
1 lb. of shell-less shrimp
1 big mango, peeled and diced
1/2 red onion, diced
4 small tomatoes, peeled and diced
1 chile serrano pepper, chopped
cilantro, to desire
1 avocado, diced
20 limes, juice

Directions
1. Get a mixing bowl: Stir in it the shrimp and salmon with lime juice. Season them with a pinch of salt.
2. Cover the bowl and place it in the fridge for 2 h 30 min.
3. Once the time is up, drain the shrimp and salmon. Transfer them to another mixing bowl.
4. Add the remaining ingredients and toss them to coat.
5. Spoon your ceviche into serving glasses and serve them.
6. Enjoy.

Bahamian Ceviche

Prep Time: 20 mins
Total Time: 20 mins

Servings per Recipe: 6
Calories   233.2
Fat   18.6g
Cholesterol   27.5mg
Sodium   69.5mg
Carbohydrates   5.4g
Protein   11.7g

Ingredients

- 2 C. conch, cleaned and diced
- 2 C. diced poached spiny lobsters
- 1/2 small red onion, diced
- 3 scallions, sliced on the diagonal
- 1/2 small red pepper, diced
- 1/2 small yellow pepper, diced
- 1/2 small green pepper, diced
- 1/2 small papaya, peeled, seeded and diced
- 2 - 4 jalapenos, chopped
- 1/2 bunch chopped cilantro
- 1/2 bunch chopped basil
- 1/2 bunch chopped mint leaves
- 1 tbsp grated fresh ginger
- 1/2 lime, juiced
- 1/4 C. rice wine vinegar
- 1/2 C. extra virgin olive oil
- salt and pepper
- 1 pinch ground habanero chile pepper

Directions

1. Get a mixing bowl: Stir in it all the ingredients.
2. Cover it and chill it in the fridge for 3 h 30 min.
3. Once the time is up, spoon your ceviche into serving glasses. Serve them with some chips.
4. Enjoy.

NEW ENGLAND
Ceviche Bowls

Prep Time: 3 hr
Total Time: 3 hr

Servings per Recipe: 4
Calories	153.3
Fat	4.5g
Cholesterol	34.0mg
Sodium	682.2mg
Carbohydrates	10.6g
Protein	17.1g

Ingredients
1 lb. clams, cleaned and chopped
1 pink grapefruit, peeled and diced
1 tsp pink peppercorns
12 mint leaves, slivered
1 tbsp extra virgin olive oil
kosher salt
tortilla chips

Directions
1. Get a mixing bowl: Stir in it all the ingredients.
2. Cover the bowl and place it in the fridge for 3 to 4 h.
3. Once the time is up, adjust the seasoning of your ceviche then serve it.
4. Enjoy.

Sunday's Ceviche

Prep Time: 15 mins
Total Time: 25 mins

Servings per Recipe: 4
Calories   236.9
Fat   10.8g
Cholesterol   56.7mg
Sodium   344.3mg
Carbohydrates   13.4g
Protein   25.0g

Ingredients

- 1 lb. tilapia fillet, cut into pieces
- 1 - 2 jalapeno pepper, minced
- 1/2 C. lime juice
- 1/2 C. fresh cilantro, chopped and divided
- 1 tsp fresh oregano, chopped
- 1/4 tsp salt
- 1 large green bell pepper, halved crosswise and sliced
- 1 large tomatoes, chopped
- 1/2 C. white onion, sliced
- 1/4 C. green olives, quartered
- 1 avocado, chopped

Directions

1. Place a pan over high heat. Place in it the fish and cover it with water. Cook it until it starts boiling.
2. Turn off the heat and cover the pan. Let the fish sit for 6 min.
3. Get a mixing bowl: Stir in it the fish after draining it with bell pepper, tomato, onion, and olives.
4. Cover the bowl and chill it in the fridge for 25 min.
5. Once the time is up, add the rest of the avocado and cilantro.
6. Adjust the seasoning of your ceviche then serve it.
7. Enjoy.

ISABELLE'S
Ceviche

🥣 Prep Time: 3 hr
🕐 Total Time: 3 hr

Servings per Recipe: 4
Calories 341.7
Fat 4.9g
Cholesterol 179.5mg
Sodium 290.3mg
Carbohydrates 30.3g
Protein 44.8g

Ingredients
2/3 lb. large shrimp, peeled and cleaned
2/3 lb. scallops, quartered
2/3 lb. salmon, skinned and pin-boned
1 tomatoes, chopped
1 mango, peeled and cubed
1/4 red onion, chopped
1 jalapeno, seeded and
1 C. lime juice
2/3 C. orange juice

1/2 C. loosely packed coriander leaves, chopped
1 tbsp powdered sugar
1 large oranges, peeled and segmented
popcorn, seasoned with chili, cumin, and salt

Directions
1. Bring a salted saucepan of water to a boil. Cook in it the shrimp for 1 min.
2. Drain it and transfer it to an ice bowl of water. Drain it again and transfer it to a mixing bowl.
3. Add to them the scallops with salmon, mango, onion, chile, lime and orange juice.
4. Cover the bowl and place it in the fridge for 3 h 30 min.
5. Once the time is up, drain the fish and transfer it to a mixing bowl.
6. Stir into them coriander, sugar, orange, and a pinch of salt. Serve your ceviche right away.
7. Enjoy.

Indonesian Ceviche

Prep Time: 15 mins
Total Time: 45 mins

Servings per Recipe: 4
Calories   178.0
Fat   7.7g
Cholesterol   37.5mg
Sodium   310.4mg
Carbohydrates   8.2g
Protein   19.6g

Ingredients

- 1 lb. sea scallops, sliced, crescent-shaped side muscles removed
- 1 C. lime juice
- 2 tbsp peanut oil
- 1 tbsp scallion, sliced
- 1 tbsp cilantro leaf, minced
- 1 1/2 tsp ginger, minced
- 1 1/2 tsp soy sauce
- 1 tsp rice vinegar
- salt and pepper

Directions

1. Get a mixing bowl: Stir in it the scallop slices with lime juice.
2. Cover it and place it in the fridge for 35 min.
3. Once the time is up, drain the scallops and transfer it to a mixing bowl.
4. Add to it the rest of the ingredients. Toss them to coat.
5. Adjust the seasoning of your ceviche then serve it.
6. Enjoy.

HOT
Cilantro Ceviche

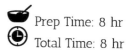
Prep Time: 8 hr
Total Time: 8 hr

Servings per Recipe: 4
Calories	153.0
Fat	2.1g
Cholesterol	172.8mg
Sodium	172.9mg
Carbohydrates	10.2g
Protein	24.0g

Ingredients
- 1 lb. small shrimp, peeled and deveined
- 2 jalapenos,
- 1 tbsp onion,
- 2 medium tomatoes, diced
- 1 tbsp cilantro, chopped
- 1 C. lime juice
- 3 tbsp lemon juice

Directions
1. Get a mixing bowl: Stir in it the shrimp with the remaining ingredients.
2. Cover it and let it chill in the fridge for 9 h.
3. Once the time is up, serve your ceviche with some crackers.
4. Enjoy.

Pickled Papaya Ceviche

Prep Time: 24 hr
Total Time: 24 hr 10 mins

Servings per Recipe: 4
Calories   240.5
Fat   0.8g
Cholesterol   18.7mg
Sodium   233.0mg
Carbohydrates   50.0g
Protein   11.6g

Ingredients

Onions
8 oz. champagne vinegar
1/2 C. sugar
2 serrano chilies, seeded
2 medium red onions, sliced
Salad
6 oz. lime juice
1/2 lb. firm white flesh fish
1/2 lb. small scallop
1 medium solo papaya, peeled seeded and diced
2 plum tomatoes, seeded and diced
4 serrano peppers, seeded and diced
1 C. Vidalia onion, diced
1/2 C. chopped cilantro
1 jalapeno chile, seeded and diced
1 tbsp white wine Worcestershire sauce
1 tbsp Mexican hot sauce
2 oz. tomato juice

Directions

1. To prepare the pickled onion:
2. Place a heavy saucepan over medium heat. Stir in it the vinegar, sugar, and chilies.
3. Heat them until they start boiling while stirring.
4. Place the onion in a heatproof container and pour over it the vinegar mixture.
5. Get a roasting dish and fill half 1/3 of it with ice cold water. Lower in it the container and let it cool down.
6. To prepare the ceviche:
7. Get a mixing bowl: Place in it the scallops and pour over the lime juice. Let them sit for 8 h in the fridge.
8. Once the time is up, drain and discard the lime juice.
9. Stir in the papaya, tomatoes, peppers, cilantro, jalapeño, Worcestershire, hot sauce, and tomato juice.
10. Spoon your ceviche into a serving plate and top it with the pink onion after draining.
11. Enjoy.

CEVICHE
Micronesia

🥣 Prep Time: 15 mins
🕐 Total Time: 15 mins

Servings per Recipe: 4
Calories 308.3
Fat 14.4g
Cholesterol 51.0mg
Sodium 95.2mg
Carbohydrates 17.5g
Protein 29.9g

Ingredients

1 lb. yellowfin tuna fillet, cubed
3/4 C. lime juice
2 tomatoes, chopped
1/2 small onion, minced
1 cucumber, diced
1 carrot, shredded
1 C. coconut milk
1 green bell pepper, sliced
spring onion
parsley

Directions

1. Get a mixing bowl: Place in it the fish and cover it with seawater or salted water. Let it sit for 10 min.
2. Once the time is up, drain the tuna and transfer it to a mixing bowl.
3. Add to it the lemon juice. Let them sit for 6 min.
4. Once the time is up, discard 2/3 of the lemon juice covering the fish.
5. Add to them the remaining ingredients. Toss them to coat.
6. Adjust the seasoning of your ceviche then serve it.
7. Enjoy.

Chicago Ceviche

Prep Time: 5 mins
Total Time: 1 hr 5 mins

Servings per Recipe: 1
Calories	228.8
Fat	18.6g
Cholesterol	33.3mg
Sodium	751.6mg
Carbohydrates	7.1g
Protein	8.6g

Ingredients
- 2 C. chopped frankfurters
- 1 C. chopped tomato
- 1/2 C. chopped white onion
- 1 jalapeno, seeded and chopped
- 1/4 C. chopped cilantro leaf
- salt
- pepper
- 2 tbsp lime juice

Directions
1. Get a mixing bowl: Stir in it all the ingredients. Cover it and refrigerate it for 60 min.
2. Once the time is up, drain your ceviche then serve it.
3. Enjoy

TANGY Mustard Ceviche

Prep Time: 30 mins
Total Time: 31 mins

Servings per Recipe: 8
Calories	218.3
Fat	1.9g
Cholesterol	220.8mg
Sodium	875.4mg
Carbohydrates	29.0g
Protein	26.5g

Ingredients

- 2 lbs. shrimp, peeled and deveined
- 10 limes, juice
- 1 lemon, large, juice
- 4 oranges, juice
- 2/3 C. ketchup
- 1 tsp mustard, regular
- 2 - 4 tbsp hot sauce
- 6 tomatoes, Roma, seeded and diced
- 2 red onions, halved and sliced
- 1/2 C. cilantro leaf, chopped
- 1 tsp salt
- 1/4 tsp black pepper

Directions

1. Place a large pan over medium heat. Heat in it 3 C. of water until they start boiling.
2. Stir in the shrimp and blanch it for 1 min. Drain it and place it aside.
3. Get a mixing bowl: Mix in it the onions, tomatoes, cilantro, and shrimp.
4. Add the remaining ingredients and toss them to coat.
5. Chill your ceviche in the fridge for 4 h then serve it.
6. Enjoy.

Bonnie's Favorite Ceviche

Prep Time: 20 mins
Total Time: 3 hr 50 mins

Servings per Recipe: 4
Calories	312.5
Fat	10.2g
Cholesterol	191.5mg
Sodium	560.2mg
Carbohydrates	25.6g
Protein	35.7g

Ingredients

- 1 lb. medium shrimp, peeled, deveined and chopped
- 1/2 lb. scallops, chopped
- 2 lemons, juiced
- 2 limes, juiced
- 1 orange, juiced
- 1 C. cucumber, peeled, seeded & diced
- 1 red onion, diced
- 1 jalapeno, diced
- 1 C. tomatoes, seeded and diced
- 1 avocado, chopped
- 1 tbsp cilantro, chopped
- 1/2 tsp salt
- 1/4 tsp cumin
- 1/8 tsp cayenne pepper

Directions

1. Get a roasting dish: Stir in it the scallops with shrimp, lemon, lime and orange juice.
2. Cover the pan and chill it in the fridge for 4 h while stirring it every 60 min.
3. Get a mixing bowl: Stir in it the cucumber, onion, jalapeno, tomatoes, avocado, cilantro, salt, cumin, and cayenne pepper.
4. Drain the fish and add it to the bowl. Pour over them some of the marinating juice to add more flavor.
5. Toss your ceviche to coat then chill in the fridge for 35 min. Serve it with some chips.
6. Enjoy.

CEVICHE
Brasileiro

🥘 Prep Time: 1 hr
🕐 Total Time: 1 hr 15 mins

Servings per Recipe: 6
Calories   544.1
Fat   31.4g
Cholesterol   92.9mg
Sodium   132.4mg
Carbohydrates   13.0g
Protein   53.5g

Ingredients

3 lbs. flank steaks
6 oz. mixed baby greens
Ceviche
2 lbs. button mushrooms
1/3 C. squeezed lemon juice
1/2 C. squeezed lime juice
1/3 C. squeezed orange juice
1/3 C. olive oil
1 red onion, sliced
1 red bell pepper, seeded, sliced
4 cloves garlic, minced
2 tbsp chopped cilantro
salt and pepper

Directions

1. Get a mixing bowl: Stir in it the mushrooms, lemon juice, orange juice, lime juice and olive oil.
2. Cover the bowl and let it sit for 60 min.
3. Once the time is up, stir in the onion, bell pepper, garlic, cilantro, salt, and pepper.
4. Cover it and let it sit in the fridge for 3 hours at least.
5. Before you do anything else, preheat the grill and grease it.
6. Season the steak with a pinch of salt and pepper. Cook it on the grill for 7 to 9 min on each side.
7. Serve it warm with the ceviche.
8. Enjoy.

Country Ceviche

Prep Time: 30 mins
Total Time: 40 mins

Servings per Recipe: 8
Calories   144.7
Fat   1.0g
Cholesterol   0.0mg
Sodium   310.6mg
Carbohydrates   32.1g
Protein   6.2g

Ingredients

- 3 ears sweet corn
- 2 - 4 garlic cloves, minced
- 1 (14 1/2 oz.) cans black beans, rinsed and drained
- 4 - 5 limes, zested and juiced
- 2 celery ribs, diced
- 1 cucumber, diced
- 3 tomatoes, diced
- 1/2 C. cilantro, chopped
- 1 - 2 jalapeno, diced
- 1/2 red onion, diced
- 1 red bell pepper, diced
- 1 green bell pepper, diced
- 1 yellow bell pepper, diced
- 1 C. pineapple, chopped
- 1 C. mango, chopped
- 1 tsp salt

Directions

1. Scrap off the kernels from the cob.
2. Place a skillet over high heat. Heat in it 1 tbsp of olive oil.
3. Cook in it the corn with garlic for 1 to 2 min. Stir in the black beans with lime juice and zest.
4. Get a mixing bowl: Stir in it the remaining ingredients with corn mix, a pinch of salt and pepper.
5. Adjust the seasoning of your ceviche then serve it with some tortilla chips.
6. Enjoy.

ORIENTAL Ceviche

Prep Time: 35 mins
Total Time: 35 mins

Servings per Recipe: 4
Calories   173.0
Fat   0.6g
Cholesterol   9.9mg
Sodium   11175.5mg
Carbohydrates   34.2g
Protein   14.1g

Ingredients

Dipping Sauce
- 2 C. fish sauce
- 3 C. lime juice
- 1/2 C. chopped cilantro
- 1/2 C. chopped basil
- 1/2 C. chopped of mint
- 1 tbsp peeled and minced ginger

Ceviche
- 8 large sea scallops, sliced into disks
- 1 C. dipping sauce
- 1/4 lb. mache or romaine lettuce
- 1 large shallot, sliced
- 1 mango, flesh removed from the pit and sliced
- 2 limes, juice
- 1 tsp pink peppercorns

Directions

1. To prepare the dipping sauce:
2. Get a mixing bowl: Whisk in it all the sauce ingredients.
3. Chill it in the fridge until ready to serve.
4. To prepare the ceviche:
5. Lay the mache leaves on a serving plate. Top each one of them with 3 scallop slices, half the shallot, and all of the mango.
6. Cover them with the remaining scallops and shallot.
7. Drizzle over them the lime juice followed by peppercorns.
8. Serve your ceviche immediately with the dipping sauce.
9. Enjoy.

Mango Ceviche Wraps

Prep Time: 10 mins
Total Time: 10 mins

Servings per Recipe: 4
Calories   260.8
Fat   14.8g
Cholesterol   18.7mg
Sodium   1221.7mg
Carbohydrates   15.3g
Protein   19.1g

Ingredients

- 250 g tuna fish, cubed
- 1 mango, cubed
- 1 avocado, cubed
- Sauce
- 4 tbsp light soy sauce
- 4 tbsp lime juice
- chili powder
- 2 tbsp olive oil
- 2 tbsp balsamic vinegar

Directions

1. Get a mixing bowl: Toss in it all the ingredients.
2. Cover it and chill it in the fridge for 1 h or serve it immediately.
3. Enjoy.

NAKED Ceviche

Prep Time: 20 mins
Total Time: 1 hr 20 mins

Servings per Recipe: 8
Calories   231.4
Fat   12.6g
Cholesterol   129.6mg
Sodium   208.7mg
Carbohydrates   12.5g
Protein   19.5g

Ingredients

- 1 1/2 lbs. raw shrimp, peeled and cleaned
- 5 limes, juice
- 2 tbsp minced jalapenos, divided
- 1/4 C. minced red onion, divided
- 1/4 tsp salt
- 1 cucumber, peeled, seeded, and diced
- 3 avocados, diced
- 2 tomatoes, seeded and diced
- 1 bunch fresh cilantro, chopped
- tortilla chips

Directions

1. Get a mixing bowl: Stir in it the shrimp with lime juice, 1 tbsp jalapeno, 2 tbsp red onion, and a pinch of salt.
2. Cover it and place it in the fridge for 60 min.
3. Once the time is up, stir in the cucumber, avocado, tomato, and cilantro.
4. Adjust the seasoning of your ceviche then serve it with some chips.
5. Enjoy.

Chipotle Ceviche

🥣 Prep Time: 20 mins
🕐 Total Time: 20 mins

Servings per Recipe: 4
Calories   164.2
Fat   11.1g
Cholesterol   9.2mg
Sodium   54.4mg
Carbohydrates   12.6g
Protein   6.7g

Ingredients

- 1/2 C. lime juice
- 1 small chili pepper, seeded and diced
- 1 tbsp extra virgin olive oil
- 1 C. sea bass, skin removed and diced
- 1 C. perch, diced
- 1 C. scallops
- 1 C. octopus, cleaned and diced
- 1/2 Spanish onion, sliced
- 1 cucumber, cut into matchsticks
- 1/4 C. fresh mint leaves
- 1/4 C. coriander, diced
- 1/4 C. parsley, diced
- 1 avocado, peeled, pitted, and diced
- 1/4 red capsicum, sliced
- salt & pepper

Directions

1. Get a mixing bowl: Stir in it the fish with lime juice.
2. Cover it and chill it in the fridge overnight.
3. Once the time is up, drain it and transfer it to a mixing bowl.
4. Add to it the remaining ingredients and toss them to coat.
5. Adjust the seasoning of your ceviche then serve it.
6. Enjoy.

CEVICHE
in Tortilla Bowls

Prep Time: 30 mins
Total Time: 1 hr 40 mins

Servings per Recipe: 5
Calories	438.4
Fat	7.7g
Cholesterol	42.5mg
Sodium	103.1mg
Carbohydrates	66.5g
Protein	32.2g

Ingredients

- 1 lb. red snapper fillet, skin removed, diced
- 1 C. diced tomatoes
- 1/2 C. diced white onion
- 1/2 C. lime juice
- 1/2 C. orange juice
- 2 tbsp chopped cilantro
- 1 tbsp olive oil
- 1 tbsp minced jalapeno
- 1 tsp grated lime zest
- 1 tsp grated orange zest
- salt & ground black pepper
- bibb lettuce, cleaned
- Tortilla Bowls
- 12 (6 inches) corn tortillas
- 4 C. corn
- salt
- Emeril's Original Essence, or Cajun spice

Directions

1. Get a large mixing bowl: Stir in it all the ingredients.
2. Layover it a plastic wrap to cover it. Chill it in the fridge for 60 min.
3. Place a heavy saucepan over high heat. Heat in it the oil.
4. Dip the tortillas in oil and drain them right away. Slice them into strips.
5. Arrange 1/5 of the strips in a ladle. Lower it into the hot oil.
6. Let them cook until the tortillas harden and become crunchy in the shape of a bowl.
7. Arrange lettuce leaves on a plate, top them with tortilla bowls, ceviche, and corn on top.
8. Enjoy.

Ceviche Wraps II

⏺ Prep Time: 20 mins
🕐 Total Time: 40 mins

Servings per Recipe: 4
Calories   646.2
Fat   30.1g
Cholesterol   154.4mg
Sodium   638.1mg
Carbohydrates   43.7g
Protein   50.0g

Ingredients

- 1 lb. firm white fish fillet, thawed and chopped
- 2/3 C. lime juice
- 12 oz. Jarlsberg cheese
- 2 limes, zest
- 1 medium tomatoes, seeded and chopped
- 2 green onions, chopped
- 4 oz. chili peppers, drained
- 1/2 C. chopped cilantro leaves
- 1 tsp ground cumin
- 4 large radishes, sliced
- 12 oil-cured olives, seeded and chopped
- 8 flour tortillas

Directions

1. Get a mixing bowl: Stir in it the fish with lime juice. Cover it and let it sit in the fridge for 35 min.
2. Once the time is up, drain it and transfer it to a mixing bowl.
3. Add to it the lime zest with tomato, onion, chili peppers, cilantro, 1/2 C. of cheese, cumin, radishes, and olives.
4. Toss them to coat. Cover the bowl and place it in the fridge.
5. Before you do anything else, preheat the oven to 375 F.
6. Spoon 1 C. of ceviche into each tortilla and roll them tightly.
7. Arrange them in a greased baking dish. Top them with cheese and cover them with a cling foil.
8. Cook it in the oven for 26 min. Discard the foil and cook it for an extra 5 min.
9. Once the time is up, serve your ceviche rolls warm.
10. Enjoy.

SOUTHWEST
Ceviche

🥣 Prep Time: 15 mins
🕐 Total Time: 4 hr 15 mins

Servings per Recipe: 4
Calories	390.2
Fat	11.1g
Cholesterol	165.3mg
Sodium	216.5mg
Carbohydrates	5.7g
Protein	64.1g

Ingredients
4 skinned salmon fillets, shredded
4 limes, juice
2 red chilies
2 tbsp coriander, chopped
1/4 tsp ground cumin
2 garlic cloves
4 cm grated fresh ginger

Directions
1. Get a mixing bowl: Stir in it the salmon with tomatoes, green pepper, celery, onion, cilantro, a pinch of salt and pepper.
2. Press the ginger to squeeze out its juice and over the fish mix.
3. Cover the bowl with a plastic wrap and chill it in the fridge for 5 h.
4. Once the time is up, serve your ceviche with some chips.
5. Enjoy.

Bethany Beach Ceviche

Prep Time: 6 hr
Total Time: 6 hr

Servings per Recipe: 6
Calories   85.8
Fat   4.9g
Cholesterol   0.0mg
Sodium   23.6mg
Carbohydrates   12.2g
Protein   1.6g

Ingredients

1 lb. fish, diced
3 limes, juice
2 tomatoes, chopped, remove seeds and juice
1 large green pepper, chopped
3 celery ribs, chopped
1 onion, chopped
1 bunch cilantro

Dressing
2 tbsp olive oil
2 limes, juice of
2 jalapenos, minced, remove seeds and ribs
2 garlic cloves,
1 tsp cayenne pepper
3/4 tsp cumin
salt and pepper

Directions

1. Get a mixing bowl: Stir in it the fish with lime juice. Cover it and let it sit in the fridge for 5 h.
2. Once the time is up, drain the fish and transfer it to a mixing bowl.
3. Stir into it the tomatoes, green pepper, celery, onion, and cilantro. Spoon it into a serving plate.
4. Get a mixing bowl: Whisk in it the dressing ingredients. Drizzle it over the ceviche then serve it.
5. Enjoy.

GREEK
Ceviche

🥣 Prep Time: 20 mins
🕐 Total Time: 2 hr 20 mins

Servings per Recipe: 4
Calories   248.3
Fat   11.2g
Cholesterol   177.1mg
Sodium   328.4mg
Carbohydrates   16.2g
Protein   26.1g

Ingredients

- 1 lb. fresh raw red shrimp, peeled, deveined and chopped
- 1/4 C. minced scallion
- 1/4 C. minced chives
- 1/4 C. julienned basil
- 3 ripe Roma tomatoes, peeled, seeded and minced
- 1/4 C. chopped kalamata olive
- 3 garlic cloves, chopped
- 3 fresh lemons, zest
- salt and pepper
- 1 tbsp seasoned breadcrumbs
- 2 tbsp feta, crumbled
- 2 tbsp extra virgin olive oil

Directions

1. Get a mixing bowl: Stir in it the srimo with scallion, chives, basil, tomato, olives, garlic, and lemon zest.
2. Season them with a pinch of salt and pepper then toss them to coat.
3. Cover the bowl and chill it in the fridge for 3 to 5 h.
4. Once the time is up, divide the ceviche between serving glasses.
5. Garnish them with breadcrumbs, feta and a drizzle of olive oil.
6. Serve them immediately.
7. Enjoy.

Vegetarian Dream Ceviche

Prep Time: 20 mins
Total Time: 2 hr 20 mins

Servings per Recipe: 6
Calories   211.2
Fat   6.8g
Cholesterol   0.0mg
Sodium   27.0mg
Carbohydrates   34.3g
Protein   14.6g

Ingredients

- 2 lbs. extra firm tofu, cubed
- 2 tbsp pickled ginger, minced
- 1 tbsp garlic, minced
- 1/2 bunch cilantro, chopped
- 10 limes, juice
- 2 lemons, juice
- 1/4 C. rice wine vinegar
- 3 tbsp sugar
- 1/2 mango, cut brunoise, cubed
- 1/2 cucumber, peeled and seeded, quartered
- 2 vine ripe tomatoes, cut brunoise, cubed
- 1/2 red onion, cut brunoise, cubed
- 2 scallions, cut diagonally
- 1/4 pineapple, cut brunoise, cubed
- 1/2 jalapeno pepper, seeded and cut brunoise, cubed

Directions

1. Get a roasting dish: Stir in it the tofu with mangoes, tomatoes, cucumbers, red onions, scallions, pineapple, and jalapenos.
2. Get a mixing bowl: Whisk in it the pickled ginger, garlic, cilantro, limes, lemons, vinegar, salt, and pepper.
3. Drizzle them over the tofu mixture and toss them to coat. Cover the pan with a cling foil and refrigerate it for 3 h.
4. Once the time is up, serve your ceviche with some tostadas.
5. Enjoy.

HASSAN'S
Harbor Ceviche

🥣 Prep Time: 30 mins
🕒 Total Time: 4 hr 30 mins

Servings per Recipe: 4
Calories　　　　　323.9
Fat　　　　　　　14.8g
Cholesterol　　　　36.5mg
Sodium　　　　　322.4mg
Carbohydrates　　43.8g
Protein　　　　　16.9g

Ingredients
1/2 lobster
1/2 lb. sea scallops, cleaned and patted dry
4 oranges, juiced
4 lemons, juiced
4 limes, juiced
1 Bermuda onion, sliced
2 small tomatoes, chopped
3 tbsp fresh cilantro, chopped
1/2 small habanero, chopped

1/4 C. Spanish olive oil
1/4 C. ketchup
salt & ground pepper
avocado
plantain chips

Directions
1. Bring a large saucepan of water to a boil. Cook in it the lobster for 6 to 7 min.
2. Drain it and place it in a bowl of ice-cold water. Drain it and transfer it to a mixing bowl.
3. Add to it the orange, lemon, and lime juice, onions, tomatoes, cilantro, habanero, olive oil, ketchup, salt, and pepper.
4. Toss them to coat. Cover the bowl with a plastic wrap and chill it in the fridge for 4 to 5 h.
5. Once the time is up, strain the ceviche then serve it with some avocado.
6. Enjoy.

Hot Ginger Ceviche

🥣 Prep Time: 30 mins
🕐 Total Time: 30 mins

Servings per Recipe: 6
Calories   184.3
Fat   7.6g
Cholesterol   190.9mg
Sodium   1059.4mg
Carbohydrates   8.0g
Protein   21.7g

Ingredients

2 lbs. raw shrimp, peeled, deveined and cut into pieces
1 whole sweet white onion
2 jalapenos
1 bunch cilantro
1 (6 oz.) cans coconut milk
2 inches ginger, peeled and chopped
1/2 tsp salt

6 limes, juice

Directions

1. Get a mixing bowl: Combine in it all the ingredients.
2. Cover the bowl and chill it in the fridge for a whole day.
3. Serve your ceviche with some chips.
4. Enjoy.

FAIRBANKS
French Ceviche

🥣 Prep Time: 2 hr
🕒 Total Time: 2 hr 5 mins

Servings per Recipe: 1
Calories	114.4
Fat	2.1g
Cholesterol	29.4mg
Sodium	104.2mg
Carbohydrates	12.2g
Protein	12.4g

Ingredients
1 lb. skinless Alaska salmon, cubed
2/3 C. squeezed lime juice
2/3 C. squeezed orange juice
1 medium red onion, chopped
1 large fresh poblano chile, blackened, peeled and chopped
2 large seedless oranges, cut into segments
2 tbsp small capers, drained
1/3 C. fresh cilantro, chopped

3 -5 leaves cilantro
salt
2 C. frisee
sliced toasted French bread

Directions
1. Get a mixing bowl: Stir in it the salmon with lime and orange juice, onion, and a pinch of salt.
2. Cover the bowl and chill it in the fridge for 3 h.
3. Once the time is up, drain the salmon and pat it dry.
4. Get a mixing bowl: Stir in it the capers with salmon, cilantro, orange segments, onion, and a pinch of salt.
5. Cover the bowl and chill it in the fridge for 30 min.
6. Spoon your ceviche into a bed of lettuce or frisee then serve it.
7. Enjoy.

Crunchy Crab Ceviche

Prep Time: 10 mins
Total Time: 20 mins

Servings per Recipe: 6
Calories   642.6
Fat   20.1g
Cholesterol   264.0mg
Sodium   1145.5mg
Carbohydrates   68.9g
Protein   47.5g

Ingredients

- canola oil
- 18 (5 inches) tortillas
- 1 1/2 lbs. medium cooked shrimp, peeled, deveined and chopped
- 3/4 lb. lump crabmeat
- 1/4 C. lemon juice
- 2 tbsp chopped cilantro
- 1 large cucumber, peeled, seeded and chopped
- 2 large tomatoes, chopped
- 1 - 2 jalapeno chile, stemmed, seeded
- 1 small red onion
- salt
- 2 avocados, peeled, seeded and sliced
- 2 limes, cut into wedges

Directions

1. Place a heavy large saucepan over medium-high heat. Heat in it 1 inch of oil.
2. Cook in it the tortillas in batches until they become crunchy and golden.
3. Drain them and transfer them to paper towels.
4. Get a mixing bowl: Stir in it the shrimp, crab, lemon juice, cilantro, cucumbers, tomatoes, jalapenos, onions, and salt.
5. Arrange your tortilla crackers on a serving plate. Spoon over them the ceviche then serve them.
6. Enjoy.

PINEAPPLE CEVICHE with Fried Cinnamon Pastry

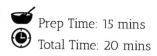

Prep Time: 15 mins
Total Time: 20 mins

Servings per Recipe: 4
Calories   597.8
Fat   35.4g
Cholesterol   0.0mg
Sodium   699.6mg
Carbohydrates   64.7g
Protein   5.5g

Ingredients

Dough
1 (15 oz.) packages Pillsbury pie crusts
cinnamon
honey
vegetable oil
Ceviche
1/4 fresh pineapple, diced
1/4 cantaloupe, diced
1/2 pint strawberry, diced

1/4 C. fresh orange juice
3 tbsp tequila, flamed to remove alcohol, optional
3 tbsp agave nectar

Directions

1. Get a mixing bowl: Wisk in it the orange juice, tequila, and nectar.
2. Add the diced fruits and toss them to coat. Chill it in the fridge for at least 3 h.
3. Place a deep skillet over medium-high heat. Heat in it 1 inch of oil.
4. Slice the pie crust into 4 pieces. Fry them in the hot oil until they become golden brown.
5. Drain them and place them on some paper towels to drain.
6. Arrange the golden pie pieces on a serving plate. Top them with some cinnamon and honey.
7. Serve them with the fruit ceviche.
8. Enjoy.

Pink Serrano Ceviche

🥣 Prep Time: 8 hr
🕐 Total Time: 8 hr 20 mins

Servings per Recipe: 4
Calories   141.5
Fat   2.3g
Cholesterol   29.4mg
Sodium   47.5mg
Carbohydrates   20.8g
Protein   12.7g

Ingredients
1/2 lb. salmon, diced
3 - 4 Roma tomatoes, diced
1 small white onion, diced
1 mango, diced
1 bunch cilantro, chopped
2 - 3 serrano peppers, diced
10 limes, juice
whole wheat crackers

Directions
1. Get a mixing bowl: Place in it the salmon and cover it with lime juice.
2. Cover the bowl and chill it in the fridge for 9 h.
3. Once the time is up, drain the salmon and transfer it to a mixing bowl.
4. Add to it the rest of the ingredients and toss them to coat. Serve it with some chips.
5. Enjoy.

KISSIMMEE KEY
Lime Ceviche

Prep Time: 10 mins
Total Time: 10 mins

Servings per Recipe: 4
Calories   277.0
Fat   4.3g
Cholesterol   81.3mg
Sodium   141.0mg
Carbohydrates   23.9g
Protein   38.6g

Ingredients
1 3/4 lbs. sea bass, cubed
1 red onion, sliced
1/2 red aji limo chile, chopped
1/2 yellow aji limo chile, chopped
16 key limes, juice
salt
1 ear corn on the cob, boiled & cut into rounds
boiled sweet potato

lettuce leaf

Directions
1. Get a mixing bowl: Stir in it the fish with lime, onion, chile and a pinch of salt.
2. Toss them to coat. Drain them right away and transfer them to a bowl with ice cubes.
3. Stir them and discard the ice cubes before they start melting.
4. Spoon your ceviche into serving plates with lettuce, sweet potato, and corn. Serve them right away.
5. Enjoy.

Ceviche Tilapia

Prep Time: 30 mins
Total Time: 30 mins

Servings per Recipe: 6
Calories   188.8
Fat   2.8g
Cholesterol   75.6mg
Sodium   470.2mg
Carbohydrates   13.2g
Protein   31.6g

Ingredients

2 lbs. tilapia fillets, cubed
8 -10 garlic cloves, chopped
1 tsp salt
1/2 tsp black pepper
2 tsp fresh cilantro, chopped
1 habanero pepper, seeded and chopped
8 -12 limes, squeezed and strained to remove pulp
1 red onion, sliced and rinsed

Directions

1. Get a large mixing bowl: Stir in it fish fillets with garlic, cilantro, pepper, lime juice, salt, and pepper.
2. Lay the onion slices on top. Place it in the fridge for 3 h.
3. Once the time is up, serve your ceviche with some lettuce, corn, and avocado.
4. Enjoy.

CEVICHE Bowls

Prep Time: 10 mins
Total Time: 10 mins

Servings per Recipe: 4
Calories 365.6
Fat 14.7g
Cholesterol 53.8mg
Sodium 83.3mg
Carbohydrates 24.7g
Protein 35.5g

Ingredients

- 20 oz. ahi tuna, cubed
- 1 fresh mango, peeled and cubed
- 1 fresh avocado, peeled and cubed
- 2 tbsp red onions, minced
- 1 tomatoes, roasted, peeled & seeded
- 1 serrano pepper, roasted, seeded & minced
- 1/2 C. lime juice
- 1/2 C. orange juice
- 1/8 C. tomato juice
- 1 dash Tabasco sauce
- 1 pinch sugar
- salt

Directions

1. Get a mixing bowl: Stir in it half of the lime, orange and tomato juice with tuna cubes.
2. Stir in the red onions, with roasted tomatoes, pepper, Tabasco sauce, sugar, and salt.
3. Place it in the fridge for at least 4 h.
4. Once the time is up, drain it and place it aside.
5. Stir them with the half of strained juices. Repeat the process with avocado.
6. Place small size mold in each plate. Press in it the mango, followed by avocado and fish mixture.
7. Pat them down and place them in the fridge for at least 2 h.
8. Once the time is up, gently remove your molds then serve your ceviche right away.
9. Enjoy.

Ceviche Gonzalez

Prep Time: 20 mins
Total Time: 8 hr 20 mins

Servings per Recipe: 4
Calories   181.7
Fat   2.2g
Cholesterol   68.1mg
Sodium   247.7mg
Carbohydrates   15.4g
Protein   27.3g

Ingredients

- 1 lb. halibut fillets, diced
- 5 - 6 limes, juice
- 1 C. diced tomato
- 1 green pepper, sweet, chopped
- 4 tbsp chopped parsley
- 1/4 tsp salt
- 1/4 tsp pepper
- 1/2 tsp oregano
- 2 jalapeno peppers, chopped
- 2 tbsp white vinegar
- 1 medium onion, chopped
- 2 tbsp cilantro, chopped
- 1 dash Tabasco sauce
- lettuce leaf
- avocado
- black olives, sliced

Directions

1. Stir the lime juice with halibut cubes in a mixing bowl.
2. Let them sit in the fridge for 8 h while stirring from time to time.
3. Once the time is up, drain the fish dices and add to it the rest of the ingredients.
4. Spoon your ceviche over some lettuce leaves then serve it.
5. Enjoy.

GARDEN
Ceviche

🥣 Prep Time: 30 mins
🕐 Total Time: 4 hr 30 mins

Servings per Recipe: 12
Calories   170.2
Fat   7.0g
Cholesterol   95.2mg
Sodium   436.4mg
Carbohydrates   18.9g
Protein   12.7g

Ingredients
2 - 3 lbs. shrimp, peeled and deveined
2 large tomatoes, diced
1 red onion, diced
1 bunch cilantro, diced
1 serrano peppers, diced
8 limes, squeezed
8 lemons, squeezed
2 oranges, squeezed
2 large avocados, diced

2 large cucumbers, peeled and diced

Directions
1. Bring a saucepan of water to a boil. Cook in it the shrimp for 60 sec.
2. Drain it and plunge it in icy water. Drain it and dice it.
3. Get a mixing bowl: Stir in it the shrimp with citrus juice. Let them sit for 120 min.
4. Stir in the red onion, tomatoes, chilies, and cilantro. Let them sit for another 120 min or more in the fridge.
5. Once the time is up, garnish your ceviche with cucumber and avocado then serve it.
6. Enjoy.

Big World Ceviche

Prep Time: 30 mins
Total Time: 32 mins

Servings per Recipe: 15
Calories   135.2
Fat   5.6g
Cholesterol   76.4mg
Sodium   426.8mg
Carbohydrates   13.8g
Protein   10.1g

Ingredients

- 2 lbs. medium shrimp, peeled, deveined and diced
- 8 limes, juice
- 8 lemons, juice
- 2 oranges, juice
- 2 (14 1/2 oz.) cans petite cut canned tomatoes
- 1 red onion, diced
- 1/2 bunch fresh cilantro, stemmed and chopped
- 1 serrano chili, chopped
- 2 large avocados, peeled, seeded, and diced
- 2 large cucumbers, peeled, seeded and diced
- 1 medium yellow bell pepper diced
- 1 medium red bell pepper, diced

Directions

1. Get a mixing bowl: Stir in it the shrimp with lime, lemon, and orange juice.
2. Place it in the fridge and let it sit for 7 h.
3. Once the time is up, add the remaining ingredients to the shrimp and toss them to coat.
4. Spoon the ceviche into serving glasses. Garnish them with some tortilla chips and avocado.
5. Let them sit for about 25 min then serve them.
6. Enjoy.

NEW YORK
Vegan Ceviche

🥣 Prep Time: 10 mins
🕐 Total Time: 10 mins

Servings per Recipe: 4
Calories   85.8
Fat   4.2g
Cholesterol   0.0mg
Sodium   430.0mg
Carbohydrates   11.3g
Protein   3.6g

Ingredients
1 (14 oz.) cans hearts of palm, cut in rings
2 large tomatoes, diced
1/2 small red onion, diced
1/2 bunch fresh cilantro, chopped
2 jalapenos, diced
2 limes, juice
1 tbsp olive oil
salt
pepper
avocado
cucumber
green bell pepper

Directions
1. Get a mixing bowl: Stir in it all the ingredients. Refrigerate it until ready to serve.
2. Spoon the ceviche into serving glasses. Garnish them with your favorite toppings.
3. Enjoy.

Easy Vegetarian Ceviche

Prep Time: 10 mins
Total Time: 15 mins

Servings per Recipe: 6
Calories   121.9
Fat   9.4g
Cholesterol   0.0mg
Sodium   9.5mg
Carbohydrates   8.6g
Protein   3.2g

Ingredients

1 lb. sliced fresh mushrooms, steamed
1 C. chopped red onion
2 C. tomatoes, diced
1 C. chopped cilantro
1 chopped habanero pepper
1/4 C. olive oil
salt and pepper
2 to 3 limes, juice

Directions

1. Get a mixing bowl: Stir in it all the ingredients.
2. Place it in the fridge for at least 1 h. Serve your ceviche with toppings of your choice.
3. Enjoy.

HOT
Ceviche with Crab

🥣 Prep Time: 15 mins
🕐 Total Time: 15 mins

Servings per Recipe: 6
Calories	105.1
Fat	0.7g
Cholesterol	31.7mg
Sodium	738.3mg
Carbohydrates	10.7g
Protein	15.0g

Ingredients
- 16 oz. crabmeat
- 1 1/2 C. cilantro, chopped
- 1/2 white onion, chopped
- 2 tomatoes, diced
- 1 seedless cucumber
- 3 limes
- 3 chopped serrano peppers
- 1 tbsp ketchup
- 1/2 C. Clamato juice

Directions
1. Get a mixing bowl; stir in it the crab meat with 2 limes, onion, tomatoes, chopped cucumber and Serrano peppers.
2. Season them with a pinch of salt. Place it in the fridge until ready to serve.
3. Get a mixing bowl: Whisk in it the ketchup, clamato and the juice of the third lime.
4. Spoon your ceviche into serving glasses. Top them with the ketchup sauce and serve them.
5. Enjoy.

Ceviche Mexicana

🥣 Prep Time: 15 mins
🕐 Total Time: 6 hr 15 mins

Servings per Recipe: 8
Calories   203.5
Fat   3.1g
Cholesterol   53.2mg
Sodium   1115.9mg
Carbohydrates   13.0g
Protein   31.3g

Ingredients

- 2 lbs. red snapper fillets, cubed
- 2 C. lemon juice
- 2 C. onions, chopped
- 1/2 C. tomato puree
- 1/2 C. tomato juice
- 1 tbsp salt
- 16 green olives, chopped
- 2 tbsp Worcestershire sauce
- 1 tsp Tabasco sauce
- 2 jalapenos, chopped
- 3 tomatoes, firm, peeled, seeded and chopped
- 2 tbsp cilantro
- avocado

Directions

1. Get a mixing bowl: Stir in it the dish cubes with lime juice. Let them sit in the fridge for 7 h.
2. Get a mixing bowl: Stir in it 2 C. chopped onion, 1/2 C. tomato puree, 1/2 C. tomato juice, 1 tbsp salt, and 16 chopped green olives.
3. Add 2 tbsp Worcestershire sauce, 1 tsp Tabasco, 2 chopped jalapenos, 3 chopped peeled and seeded tomatoes, and 2 tbsp cilantro.
4. Combine them well. Place it in the fridge for 7hrh.
5. Drain the fish and add it to the onion mixture. Toss them to coat.
6. Add 1 C. of the strained lime juice and combine them. Refrigerate overnight then serve it.
7. Enjoy.

PORTUGUESE
Ceviche

Prep Time: 15 mins
Total Time: 15 mins

Servings per Recipe: 6
Calories	≈150 kcal
Fat	125.5
Cholesterol	4.0g
Sodium	27.2mg
Carbohydrates	740.6mg
Protein	8.6g

Ingredients
- 2 lbs. bay scallops, halved
- 3/4 C. fresh lemon juice
- 3/4 C. fresh lime juice
- 1/2 C. red onion, slivered
- 1/2 C. yellow bell pepper, slivered
- 1 C. pimento stuffed olive, halved
- 2 tbsp olive oil
- 1 tbsp fresh cilantro, chopped
- 3 slices lime peel
- 1 tsp salt
- 3 dashes hot red pepper sauce

Directions
1. Get a roasting dish. Stir in it all the ingredients.
2. Layover it a cling foil to cover it. Refrigerate it overnight.
3. Once the time is up, spoon your ceviche into serving glasses. Garnish them with your favorite toppings
4. Enjoy.

Orange Ceviche

Prep Time: 15 mins
Total Time: 3 hr 45 mins

Servings per Recipe: 6
Calories	177.2
Fat	10.1g
Cholesterol	56.8mg
Sodium	368.4mg
Carbohydrates	12.1g
Protein	11.1g

Ingredients

- 1/2 lb. medium shrimp, peeled and deveined and chopped
- 1/2 lb. bay scallop
- 2 lemons, juice
- 2 limes, juice
- 2 oranges, juice
- 1 C. cucumber, peeled and diced
- 1/4 C. red onion, chopped
- 1 C. diced tomato
- 1 avocado, peeled, seeded, and chopped
- 1 tbsp roughly chopped cilantro leaf
- 2 tbsp extra virgin olive oil
- 1/2 tsp salt
- 1/2 tsp lemon pepper

Directions

1. Get a mixing bowl: Stir in it the lemon, lime and orange juices.
2. Add the shrimp, scallops, cucumber and red onion. Toss them to coat. Place it in the fridge for 3 h 30 min.
3. Once the time is up, add the tomato, avocado, chopped cilantro, and olive oil. Toss them to coat.
4. Spoon your ceviche into serving glasses.
5. Enjoy.

WEEKEND
Ceviche

🥣 Prep Time: 30 mins
🕐 Total Time: 1 d 30 mins

Servings per Recipe: 4
Calories   238.1
Fat   2.8g
Cholesterol   286.4mg
Sodium   1648.7mg
Carbohydrates   20.0g
Protein   33.5g

Ingredients
4 large tomatoes, diced
2 lbs. medium shrimp, peeled and deveined
1 onion, diced
1 bunch cilantro, diced
1 jalapeno, diced
12 lemons, squeezed
8 tbsp ketchup
1 tsp Worcestershire sauce
salt and pepper

Directions
1. Bring a large saucepan of water to a boil. Cook in it the shrimp for 4 to 6 min.
2. Drain it and plunge it in some ice water. Drain it and transfer it to a mixing bowl.
3. Add to it the lemon juice and stir them. Place it in the fridge for 2 to 3 h.
4. Once the time is up, stir in the salt, pepper, Ketchup, Worcestershire sauce, onion, tomatoes, chilies, and cilantro.
5. Let them sit for another 2 to 3 h in the fridge. Serve your ceviche right away with some chips.
6. Enjoy.

Sao Paulo Ceviche Toppers

Prep Time: 15 mins
Total Time: 12 hr 15 mins

Servings per Recipe: 10
Calories 646.8
Fat 9.3g
Cholesterol 138.2mg
Sodium 1305.0mg
Carbohydrates 102.2g
Protein 35.5g

Ingredients
- 1/2 small red onion, chopped
- 2 garlic cloves
- 1/4 C. chopped of mint, plus about 30 leaves of fresh mint
- 1/2 C. fresh lime juice
- salt & ground black pepper
- 2 lbs. shrimp, peeled and deveined with tail shells intact
- 30 slices French baguettes
- 1 1/2 tbsp extra virgin olive oil

Directions
1. Stir the onions, 1 clove minced garlic, chopped mint, lime juice, salt and pepper in an airtight container.
2. Stir into it them the shrimp. Cover it and place it in the fridge for 13 h while stirring it from time to time.
3. Before you do anything, preheat the oven to 350 F.
4. Once the time is up, slice the clove of garlic in half and coat it with it the bread slices.
5. Lay them on a baking tray and toast them for 10 to 16 min in the oven.
6. Allow the bread slices to cool down for few minutes then spoon into them the ceviche.
7. Drizzle over them some olive oil then serves them.
8. Enjoy.

MANGO
Salsa Ceviche

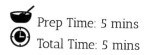

Prep Time: 5 mins
Total Time: 5 mins

Servings per Recipe: 2
Calories 116.4
Fat 7.6g
Cholesterol 0.0mg
Sodium 9.7mg
Carbohydrates 12.9g
Protein 2.5g

Ingredients

1 C. cooked shrimp, peeled and deveined
1 cucumber, peeled and diced
1 tomatoes, diced
1/2 avocado, diced
1/4 C. prepared mango salsa, see appendix
1/2 lime, juice
salt and pepper

Directions

1. Get a mixing bowl: Stir in it all the ingredients. Place it in the fridge for at least 2 h.
2. Serve it with some crackers.
3. Enjoy.

Michelle's Citrus Ceviche

Prep Time: 5 mins
Total Time: 50 mins

Servings per Recipe: 1
Calories	147.3
Fat	1.4g
Cholesterol	143.2mg
Sodium	1562.8mg
Carbohydrates	17.5g
Protein	17.0g

Ingredients

- 1 large tomatoes, halved, seeds removed
- 2 jalapeno peppers, halved, seeds removed
- 1 red bell pepper, halved, seeds removed
- 1/2 yellow onion, peeled
- 1 lb. medium shrimp, deveined, peeled, halved lengthwise
- 3/4 C. lime juice, squeezed
- 1/2 C. orange juice, squeezed
- 1/4 C. tomato juice
- 1 tbsp sugar
- 1 1/2 tsp kosher salt,
- Tabasco sauce
- 2 tbsp chives, chopped
- 2 tbsp scallions, sliced
- 1/4 C. cilantro, chopped

Directions

1. Before you do anything, preheat the oven to 500 F.
2. Cover a baking dish with a piece of foil. Lay in it the tomato, jalapenos, bell pepper and onion.
3. Cook them in the oven for 32 min. Place them aside to lose heat completely then peel them.
4. Place a large saucepan of water over high heat. Bring it to a boil.
5. Cook in it the shrimp for 2 min. Drain it and place it in some icy water. Drain it again.
6. Get a food processor: Combine in it the roasted veggies with lime juice, orange juice, tomato juice, sugar, and salt.
7. Process them until they become smooth to make the sauce.
8. Get a mixing bowl: Stir in it the shrimp with sauce, a pinch of salt and pepper.
9. Place it in the fridge for at least 1 h. Serve it with some chips.
10. Enjoy.

CORN AND RADISH
Ceviche Salad

🥣 Prep Time: 15 mins
🕐 Total Time: 19 mins

Servings per Recipe: 2
Calories　　　　353.7
Fat　　　　　　19.2g
Cholesterol　　 26.9mg
Sodium　　　　53.3mg
Carbohydrates　29.0g
Protein　　　　22.1g

Ingredients
5 oz. tuna, drained
1 ear of corn, steamed
1 cucumber, diced
4 radishes, diced
1 serrano pepper, diced
1/2 medium onion, diced
1 tomatoes, diced
1 medium avocado, diced
1 tbsp lemons

salt
pepper

Directions
1. Get a mixing bowl: Scrap into it the corn with the remaining ingredients. Toss them to coat.
2. Place it in the fridge and let it sit for 1 h.
3. Serve your ceviche with some toast or crackers.
4. Enjoy.

Cynthia's Yam Ceviche

Prep Time: 30 mins
Total Time: 1 hr

Servings per Recipe: 4
Calories   223.1
Fat   1.9g
Cholesterol   109.0mg
Sodium   271.5mg
Carbohydrates   16.5g
Protein   36.3g

Ingredients

- 3 fish fillets, cubed
- 12 cooked shrimp, cooled
- 1 red aji limo chile
- 1 yellow aji limo chile
- 1 1/2 C. lime juice
- 1 cooked sweet potato
- 1/4 bunch cilantro
- 1/2 red onion, sliced
- sea salt
- 6 ice cubes
- 1 C. white corn kernels

Directions

1. Slice off the bottom of the aji chili and rub a mixing bowl with it.
2. Dice it and place it aside. Stir the fish with 6 ice cubes, a pinch of salt and lime juice into the mixing bowl.
3. Let them sit for 16 min. Discard the ice cubes and add the shrimp with aji chili, cilantro, and red onion.
4. Place it in the fridge for another 16 min. Serve it along with corn and sweet potato.
5. Enjoy.

CEVICHE
Medellin

🥣 Prep Time: 30 mins
🕐 Total Time: 30 mins

Servings per Recipe: 6
Calories　　　　256.8
Fat　　　　　　7.8g
Cholesterol　　75.6mg
Sodium　　　　85.9mg
Carbohydrates　22.2g
Protein　　　　32.5g

Ingredients

2 lbs. tilapia fillets, sushi-grade, diced
15 limes, 14 halved, 1 cut into wedges
1/2 C. chopped seeded tomatoes
1/2 C. chopped seeded cucumber
1/3 C. chopped onion
1/4 C. chopped fresh cilantro
salt & ground black pepper
1/2 C. Clamato juice
1 tbsp bottled hot sauce

tostadas
mayonnaise
1 avocado, halved pitted, peeled, and sliced

Directions

1. Get a mixing bowl: Stir in it fish with lime juice. Place it in the fridge and let it sit for 16 min.
2. Strain it and add to it the tomato, cucumber, onion, and cilantro with the fish.
3. Sprinkle over them some salt and pepper. Toss them to coat.
4. Stir in the clam-tomato juice and the hot sauce.
5. Coat one side of the tostadas with some mayo then top them with the ceviche.
6. Garnish them with avocado then serve them.
7. Enjoy.

Ceviche with Spiced Bass

Prep Time: 15 mins
Total Time: 15 mins

Servings per Recipe: 2
Calories	505.5
Fat	31.8g
Cholesterol	93.0mg
Sodium	745.7mg
Carbohydrates	13.1g
Protein	43.0g

Ingredients

- 1 lb. filet of fresh sea bass, cubed
- 1/2 C. lime juice, squeezed
- 1/2 C. lemon juice, squeezed
- 1/4 C. red onion, chopped
- 1/4 C. red bell pepper, minced
- 1/4 C. parsley, chopped
- 1/2 C. fresh cilantro, chopped
- 1/4 C. olive oil
- 1/2 tsp sea salt
- 1/4 tsp ground pepper
- 1/8 tsp cayenne pepper

Directions

1. Get a mixing bowl: Stir in it the dish with lime and lemon juice.
2. Refrigerate it for 60 min. Stir in it the onions, red bell peppers, parsley, and cilantro.
3. Put on the lid and place it in the fridge for 120 min.
4. Once the time is up, stir in the olive oil, salt, and pepper. Serve it right away.
5. Enjoy.

HAWAIIAN
Meridian Ceviche

🥣 Prep Time: 20 mins
🕐 Total Time: 8 hr 20 mins

Servings per Recipe: 4
Calories   215.2
Fat   2.7g
Cholesterol   131.7mg
Sodium   807.3mg
Carbohydrates   14.7g
Protein   33.1g

Ingredients

12 oz. sea bass, cut into pieces
6 oz. sea scallops, cut into pieces
6 oz. shrimp, blanched and cut into pieces
1 small red onion, peeled, diced fine
2 jalapenos, diced
1 medium cucumber, peeled, diced
1 yellow bell pepper, seeded, diced
1 tsp sea salt
1/2 C. lime juice

1/4 C. lemon juice
1/4 C. pineapple juice
lime wedge
pineapple
tortilla chips

Directions

1. Get a mixing bowl: Stir in it the fish, seafood, and half of the diced veggies with salt and all three juices.
2. Toss them to coat. Place them in the fridge overnight while stirring them from time to time.
3. Once the time is up, stir in the rest of the veggies. Chill them in the fridge for 60 min.
4. Spoon the ceviche into serving glasses. Garnish them with some lime wedges then serve them.
5. Enjoy.

15-Minute Canned Ceviche

Prep Time: 15 mins
Total Time: 15 mins

Servings per Recipe: 2
Calories	263.8
Fat	16.2g
Cholesterol	35.7mg
Sodium	325.7mg
Carbohydrates	8.9g
Protein	21.1g

Ingredients

- 1 (6 oz.) cans solid white tuna packed in water, drained
- 1 fresh jalapeno chile, seeded and minced
- 1 small red onion, peeled and chopped
- 1 ripe tomatoes, diced
- 1 tbsp chopped fresh cilantro
- salt
- ground black pepper
- 1/4 C. fresh lime juice
- 2 - 3 tbsp extra-virgin olive oil
- lettuce
- fresh cilantro stem

Directions

1. Place the tuna in a mixing bowl. Top it with the chile and onion. Let them sit for 5 min.
2. Mix in the tomato, chopped cilantro, and salt and pepper. Stir in the oil with lime juice.
3. Combine them well. Place it in the fridge until ready to serve.
4. Serve your ceviche with some lettuce leaves.
5. Enjoy.

PERUVIAN
Lunch Box Wraps

🥣 Prep Time: 2 hr 15 mins
🕐 Total Time: 2 hr 15 mins

Servings per Recipe: 6
Calories   46.7
Fat   0.4g
Cholesterol   73.6mg
Sodium   90.7mg
Carbohydrates   2.2g
Protein   8.3g

Ingredients

1/2 lb. small baby shrimp, cooked
1/2 C. red radish, sliced and cut into matchsticks
1 tbsp red onion, minced
1 tbsp red pepper, minced
1/2 C. green onion, sliced on the diagonal
2 tbsp lime juice
1 tbsp cilantro, chopped
2 tsp Asian chili paste

1/2 C. summer slicing tomatoes, diced
avocado
lettuce leaf,
salt & ground black pepper

Directions

1. Get a mixing bowl: Place in it the shrimp, radish, red pepper, red and green onions.
2. Drizzle over it the lime juice and toss them to coat. Put on the lid and chill it in the fridge for 120 min.
3. Once the time is up, add the cilantro, and chili paste. Mix them well.
4. Spoon your ceviche into lettuce leaves. Arrange over them some avocado slices, and tomato then serves them.
5. Enjoy.

Ceviche Casablanca

Prep Time: 10 mins
Total Time: 30 mins

Servings per Recipe: 6
Calories   597.1
Fat   38.6g
Cholesterol   0.0mg
Sodium   687.2mg
Carbohydrates   53.2g
Protein   11.2g

Ingredients

- 3 (15 1/2 oz.) cans garbanzo beans
- 1/3 C. cider vinegar
- 1 C. olive oil
- 1 chopped onion
- 2 -3 tbsp chopped parsley
- 2 tsp dried oregano leaves
- 3 garlic cloves, minced
- 1 tbsp ketchup
- 1 1/2 C. chopped and fried beef spicy sausages
- 1 (6 oz.) can baby corn, drained and sliced
- salt
- cayenne pepper

Directions

1. Get a mixing bowl: Stir in it all the ingredients.
2. Place it in the fridge and let it sit for at least 3 h.
3. Once the time is up, serve your ceviche with chips.
4. Enjoy.

"DEVILED" Mushrooms

Prep Time: 4 hr 30 mins
Total Time: 4 hr 30 mins

Servings per Recipe: 4
Calories   431.1
Fat   32.3g
Cholesterol   83.3mg
Sodium   210.9mg
Carbohydrates   14.6g
Protein   23.9g

Ingredients

- 3/4 lb. scallops, chopped
- 1/4 lb. small baby shrimp, precooked
- 20 green peppercorns, crushed
- 1 avocado, mashed
- 2 tbsp diced scallions
- 1 summer slicing tomatoes
- 1/4 C. zucchini, diced
- 20 button mushrooms, stemmed and cleaned
- 1/4 C. sweet peas, frozen
- 1/4 C. vegetable oil
- 3 tbsp peanut oil
- 2 tsp garlic
- 2 tbsp lemon juice
- 1/2 C. lime juice
- salt and pepper

Directions

1. Get a mixing bowl: Stir in it the lime juice, peanut oil, crushed peppercorns, tomato, zucchini and frozen peas.
2. Stir in the scallops with shrimp. Put on the lid and chill it in the fridge for 3 h.
3. Once the time is up, stir in the mashed avocado with scallions into the shrimp mixture.
4. Chill it in the fridge for 35 min.
5. Get a mixing bowl: Whisk in it the vegetable oil, lemon juice, garlic, salt, and pepper.
6. Brush the inside of the mushroom with this mix.
7. Spoon into them the ceviche and serve them.
8. Enjoy.

Weeknight Ceviche

Prep Time: 15 mins
Total Time: 35 mins

Servings per Recipe: 2
Calories   317.0
Fat   21.6g
Cholesterol   44.6mg
Sodium   386.0mg
Carbohydrates   22.1g
Protein   13.3g

Ingredients

- 8 -10 large scallops, quartered
- 8 -10 large shrimp, cut
- 4 garlic cloves, minced
- kosher salt
- black pepper
- 1/4 C. cilantro, chopped
- 1 fresh jalapeno pepper, seeded and chopped
- 3/4 C. lime juice, squeezed
- 1/2 red onion, sliced salted and rinsed
- 1 C. cherry tomatoes, halved
- 2 tbsp olive oil
- 2/3 C. avocado
- 1/3 C. cilantro
- 1/3 C. water
- 1 tsp coriander

Directions

1. Place the onion slices in a mixing bowl. Season them with a pinch of salt and let them sit for 16 min.
2. Get a mixing bowl: Combine in it the shrimps, scallops, garlic, onion, salt, pepper, chili, and lime juice.
3. Place it in the fridge and let it sit for 25 min.
4. Once the time is up, stir in the cilantro, cucumber and tomato and a drizzle of olive oil. Season them with a pinch of salt.
5. Get a blender: Place in it the avocados, 1/3 C. cilantro, water, 1 tbsp olive oil, salt & pepper, coriander, 1/8 C. lime juice and 2 garlic cloves.
6. Blend them smooth to make the sauce.
7. Spoon your ceviche into some toasted bread slices or serving glasses.
8. Drizzle over them the avocado sauce then serve them.
9. Enjoy.

CEVICHE
with Prawns

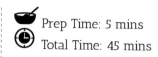

Prep Time: 5 mins
Total Time: 45 mins

Servings per Recipe: 4
Calories 261.5
Fat 16.8g
Cholesterol 142.8mg
Sodium 2383.1mg
Carbohydrates 13.1g
Protein 17.3g

Ingredients

Ceviche
1 lb. (2 to 3 dozen) prawns, peeled and diced
3 - 4 tbsp olive oil
3 tbsp chopped chives
1 tbsp sea salt
1 tbsp ground black pepper
3 limes, juice
1 jalapeno, diced
1 small yellow bell pepper, halved, seeded, white fibers removed and diced
1/2 English cucumber, diced
1/2 small shallot, chopped
3 tbsp coconut milk
Avocado
1 Hass avocado, halved, pitted and peeled
sea salt
ground black pepper
1 lime, halved

Directions

1. Get a mixing bowl: Stir in it the prawns, olive oil, chives, salt, pepper, lime juice, jalapenos, bell peppers, cucumbers, shallots and coconut milk.
2. Sprinkle over them a pinch of salt and pepper. Let them sit for 8 min in the fridge.
3. Get a mixing bowl: Mash in it the avocado slightly. Add to it the lime juice with a pinch of salt and pepper.
4. Mix them well.
5. Spoon the ceviche to a serving plate. Place next to it the mashed avocado and some fries of your choice.
6. Enjoy.

New England Ceviche with Plantains

Prep Time: 5 mins
Total Time: 40 mins

Servings per Recipe: 1
Calories   2498.5
Fat   240.3g
Cholesterol   0.0mg
Sodium   41.2mg
Carbohydrates   99.7g
Protein   5.2g

Ingredients

Ceviche
3 oz. lime juice
1 spiny lobster tail, de-shelled, deveined, cleaned, sliced
kosher salt
3 oz. julienned tomatoes
2 oz. coconut cream
2 oz. coconut milk
1/4 tsp crushed red pepper flakes
1 pinch sugar
Tostones
1 C. vegetable oil
1 green plantain, cut into 4 pieces

Directions

1. Get a mixing bowl: Stir in it the lobster with 2 oz. of lime juice, and a pinch of salt. Let it sit for 12 min.
2. Once the time is up, stir in the scallions with tomatoes, coconut cream, coconut milk, remaining lime juice, a pinch salt, the red pepper flakes and the sugar.
3. Place it in the fridge and let it sit for at least 30 min.
4. Place a pan over medium heat. Heat in it the oil. Cook in it the plantain slices until they become golden.
5. Press them slightly until they become flat. Fry them again until they become golden.
6. Serve your ceviche with plantain fries.
7. Enjoy.

CEVICHE
with Trout

🥣 Prep Time: 1 hr
🕐 Total Time: 1 hr

Servings per Recipe: 12
Calories 62.2
Fat 2.5g
Cholesterol 21.9mg
Sodium 21.7mg
Carbohydrates 1.5g
Protein 8.0g

Ingredients
1 lb. trout, trimmed and cubed
4 oz. lime juice
1-oz apple cider vinegar
1 serrano pepper, sliced
2 oz. red onions, sliced
1 medium garlic clove, sliced
1-oz fresh dill

Directions
1. Get a large mixing bowl: Combine in it all the ingredients. Toss them to coat.
2. Cover the bowl and place it in the fridge and let them sit for 16 min.
3. Once the time is up, drain the ceviche then serve it with some crackers.
4. Enjoy.

Ceviche Jamaican

Prep Time: 20 mins
Total Time: 2 hr 20 mins

Servings per Recipe: 4
Calories   194.6
Fat   2.1g
Cholesterol   214.5mg
Sodium   2714.3mg
Carbohydrates   24.8g
Protein   25.3g

Ingredients

1 1/2 lbs. large raw shrimp, peeled and deveined
10 limes, juice
1 1/2 regular size orange habaneros
1/2 of a purple onion, sliced
1 medium-size cucumber, diced
ice
3 tsp sea salt

Directions

1. Bring a large salted pot of water to a boil. Blanch in it the shrimp for 1 min.
2. Drain it and plunge it into a bowl with icy water. Drain it, and chop each one into 3 pieces.
3. Get in a mixing bowl: Stir in it the onion with cucumber and a pinch of salt. Place it in the fridge.
4. Get a blender: Combine in it the lime juice with habaneros. Blend them smooth.
5. Pour the mixture over the shrimp with a pinch of salt. Toss them to coat.
6. Place it in the fridge and let it sit for at least 120 min.
7. Once the time is up, add the onion with cucumber to the shrimp. Toss them to coat.
8. Serve your ceviche with some crackers.
9. Enjoy.

CEVICHE
Kabobs

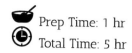

Prep Time: 1 hr
Total Time: 5 hr

Servings per Recipe: 1
Calories 21.0
Fat 0.2g
Cholesterol 6.7mg
Sodium 12.1mg
Carbohydrates 0.6g
Protein 3.8g

Ingredients
2 lbs. red snapper, cubed
1-pint grape tomatoes halved
1 large red onion, dice
2 tbsp fresh lime juice
2 tbsp pineapple juice
1 tsp fresh cilantro, minced
1 tsp shallot, minced
1 tsp jalapeno pepper, seeded, membraned
2 tbsp seasoned rice vinegar
1 pinch cayenne

Directions
1. Get a mixing bowl: Whisk in it the lime juice, pineapple juice, and rice vinegar.
2. Stir in the shallot, jalapeno, cilantro, and cayenne. Mix them well to make the marinade.
3. Get a zip lock bag: Place in it the fish, onion, and grape tomato. Pour over them the marinade.
4. Seal the bag and shake them to coat. Place it in the fridge for 5 h while shaking it every 40 min.
5. Once the time is up, drain the tomato with onion and fish from the marinade.
6. Thread them onto wooden skewers then serve them.
7. Enjoy.

Ceviche Autumn

Prep Time: 4 hr 15 mins
Total Time: 4 hr 15 mins

Servings per Recipe: 2
Calories   395.7
Fat   11.4g
Cholesterol   86.2mg
Sodium   98.8mg
Carbohydrates   19.1g
Protein   54.9g

Ingredients

- 1 lb. fresh tuna
- 3 lemons, juice
- 3 limes, juice
- 1 garlic clove, minced
- 1 small red onion, minced
- 1 jalapeno, chopped
- 2 tbsp chopped cilantro
- 2 tbsp parsley
- 2 small firm-fleshed tomatoes, chopped
- salt
- 1 avocado, sliced

Directions

1. Get a large bowl of water. Stir in it 1 tsp of salt with fish. Let it sit for 12 min.
2. Drain it, dry it and dice it. Place it in the shallow dish then top it with onion.
3. Get a mixing bowl: Whisk in it the remaining ingredients. Pour them over the onion and fish.
4. Cover the dish and place it in the fridge for 5 h while stirring every hour. Serve it with some avocado.
5. Enjoy.

KIARA'S Mint Ginger Ceviche

Prep Time: 20 mins
Total Time: 1 hr 20 mins

Servings per Recipe: 6
Calories 109.7
Fat 3.1g
Cholesterol 147.2mg
Sodium 172.3mg
Carbohydrates 3.7g
Protein 16.4g

Ingredients

1/4 C. squeezed lime juice
1 jalapeno pepper, seeded and diced
1 tsp grated ginger
1 tbsp extra virgin olive oil
1 lb. shrimp, skins removed and diced
3 scallions, white and light-green parts only, sliced on the bias
1 cucumber, cut into matchsticks
1/4 C. fresh mint leaves
1/4 C. fresh cilantro leaves
1 avocado, peeled, pitted, and diced
salt & ground black pepper

Directions

1. Get a bowl: Whisk in it the juice, jalapeño, ginger, and oil. Stir in the shrimp.
2. Cover the bowl with a cling foil and place it in the fridge overnight.
3. Once the time is up, stir in the remaining ingredients.
4. Adjust the seasoning of your ceviche then serve it.
5. Enjoy.

6-Ingredient Ceviche

Prep Time: 2 hr
Total Time: 2 hr

Servings per Recipe: 6
Calories   115.3
Fat   1.4g
Cholesterol   183.4mg
Sodium   450.3mg
Carbohydrates   9.8g
Protein   16.9g

Ingredients

1 lb. fresh uncooked shrimp, peeled and chopped
1/2 lb. fresh uncooked squid, chopped
2 medium tomatoes, chopped
1 bunch fresh cilantro, chopped
10 limes, juice
salt and pepper

Directions

1. Get a mixing bowl: Stir in it the shrimp with squid, lime juice.
2. Cover it and place it in the fridge for 2 h.
3. Once the time is up, stir in the cilantro with tomato, a pinch of salt and pepper.
4. Cover the bowl with a cling foil and place it in the fridge for at least 5 h.
5. Serve it with some crackers.
6. Enjoy.

AMERICAN
Ceviche

🥣 Prep Time: 30 mins
🕐 Total Time: 1 hr

Servings per Recipe: 4
Calories	279.5
Fat	4.1g
Cholesterol	37.5mg
Sodium	1557.5mg
Carbohydrates	43.7g
Protein	22.6g

Ingredients
- 1 lb. sea scallops, rinsed
- 8 limes, juice
- 1 1/4 C. chopped onions
- 1/2 C. Spanish olives, pits removed and sliced into quarters
- 2 tbsp olive brine, from the jar
- 3 tomatoes, peeled and chopped
- 1 (14 oz.) bottles Heinz hot ketchup
- 1 tbsp crumbled dried oregano

Directions
1. Get a mixing bowl: Stir in it the scallops with lime juice.
2. Cover the bowl with a cling foil and place it in the fridge for 4 h.
3. Get a mixing bowl: Stir in it the remaining ingredients to make the sauce.
4. Cover it and place it in the fridge until ready to serve.
5. Drain the scallops and add them to the sauce. Toss them to coat.
6. Cover the bowl and place it in the fridge for 1 h. Serve it with some crackers.
7. Enjoy.

Florida Summer Ceviche

Prep Time: 15 mins
Total Time: 8 hr 15 mins

Servings per Recipe: 10
Calories   113.3
Fat   0.7g
Cholesterol   10.9mg
Sodium   417.0mg
Carbohydrates   21.4g
Protein   7.4g

Ingredients

- 1 lb. sea scallops, quartered
- 5 limes, juice
- 1/2 C. raspberry vinegar
- 1 tsp kosher salt
- 1 tsp black pepper
- 2 green bell peppers
- 2 yellow bell peppers
- 2 red bell peppers, seeded and diced
- 1 1/2 red onions, diced
- 2 - 3 mangoes, diced
- 6 plum tomatoes, seeded and diced
- 4 tbsp fresh cilantro, chopped
- tortilla chips
- cracker

Directions

1. Get a mixing bowl: Stir in it the scallops, lime juice, vinegar, salt, and pepper.
2. Cover the bowl with a plastic wrap. Place it in the fridge for 8 h.
3. Once the time is up, stir in the remaining ingredients.
4. Adjust the seasoning of your ceviche then serve it with some chips.
5. Enjoy.

HOT
Central American Ceviche

🥣 Prep Time: 30 mins
🕐 Total Time: 4 hr 30 mins

Servings per Recipe: 8
Calories 180.2
Fat 8.5g
Cholesterol 26.6mg
Sodium 126.2mg
Carbohydrates 11.5g
Protein 16.6g

Ingredients
1 lb. fresh skinless red snapper fillets
1 1/2 C. fresh lime juice
1 medium white onion, chopped
2 medium tomatoes, chopped
1 -3 fresh hot green chili pepper, stemmed, seeded and chopped
1/3 C. chopped cilantro
1/3 C. chopped pitted green olives
1 -2 tbsp extra virgin olive oil
salt
3 tbsp orange juice
2 small avocados, peeled, pitted and diced
tostadas

Directions
1. Get a serving glass dish. Stir in it the onion with fish and lime juice.
2. Cover it with a plastic wrap and let it sit for 5 h in the fridge.
3. Once the time is up, drain it and transfer it to a mixing bowl.
4. Add to it the tomatoes, green chilies, cilantro, olives, olive oil, a pinch of salt and pepper. Toss them to coat.
5. Stir in the orange juice and cover the bowl with a plastic wrap. Place it in the fridge for 1 h.
6. Once the time is up, garnish it with avocado then serve it.
7. Enjoy.

Ceviche Siestas

Prep Time: 15 mins
Total Time: 1 hr 15 mins

Servings per Recipe: 6
Calories 207.3
Fat 11.6g
Cholesterol 41.5mg
Sodium 790.3mg
Carbohydrates 8.8g
Protein 18.8g

Ingredients

Ceviche
1 lb. fish fillet
3/4 C. lime juice, squeezed, strained
1 1/2 tsp salt
1/2 tsp dried oregano, crumbled
Sauce
1 C. fresh basil
1 C. flat leaf parsley
1/4 C. fresh cilantro leaves
15 fresh mint leaves
1 jalapeno, sliced
1 garlic clove, sliced
1/2 tsp sugar
Garnishes
20 green olives, pitted and halved
1/2 white onion
2 tbsp olive oil
1 lime, juice
salt, if needed
1 avocado, ripe, sliced

Directions

1. Get a glass dish: Combine in it the fish with lime juice, oregano, and salt.
2. Cover it and place it in the fridge for 60 min.
3. Get a food processor: Place in it all the sauce ingredients with 1 C. of water. Blend them smooth.
4. Drain the fish and place it in a serving dish. Add to it the sauce with olives, onion, olive oil and lime juice.
5. Season them with a pinch of salt and toss them to coat. Place it aside for 25 min.
6. Once the time is up, garnish your ceviche with your favorite toppings then serve it.
7. Enjoy.

MY FIRST
Ceviche

Prep Time: 30 mins
Total Time: 30 mins

Servings per Recipe: 6
Calories   123.5
Fat   9.9g
Cholesterol   0.0mg
Sodium   7.9mg
Carbohydrates   9.7g
Protein   1.9g

Ingredients

4 Roma tomatoes, seeded, chopped
2 avocados, pitted, peeled, chopped
1/2 white onion, chopped
2 jalapenos, seeded, chopped
1/2 C. cilantro, large stems removed, chopped
1 lime

salt
1/2 lb. cooked shrimp, tail-off, shelled, deveined, cut into pieces

Directions

1. Get a mixing bowl: Stir in it the all the ingredients.
2. Season them with a pinch of salt and toss them to coat.
3. Cover the bowl and place them in the fridge for 20 min.
4. Once the time is up, serve your ceviche with some crackers.
5. Enjoy.

10-Minute Tortilla Ceviche

Prep Time: 5 mins
Total Time: 10 mins

Servings per Recipe: 4
Calories 143.0
Fat 3.0g
Cholesterol 37.4mg
Sodium 383.6mg
Carbohydrates 6.7g
Protein 22.3g

Ingredients

- 2 jalapenos, seeded and chopped
- 2 (6 oz.) cans albacore tuna in water, drained and broken up
- 1 bunch cilantro, chopped
- 1 large tomatillo, chopped
- 2 large firm tomatoes, chopped
- 2 lemons, juice
- 1 dash sea salt
- corn tortilla chips

Directions

1. Get a mixing bowl: Stir in it all the ingredients.
2. Place it in the fridge and let it sit for 25 min.
3. Once the time is up, serve it with some toasted bread or crackers.
4. Enjoy.

CEVICHE
Scoops

🥣 Prep Time: 15 mins
🕒 Total Time: 8 hr 15 mins

Servings per Recipe: 4
Calories   91.7
Fat   0.8g
Cholesterol   110.4mg
Sodium   159.5mg
Carbohydrates   8.6g
Protein   12.9g

Ingredients

1/2-3/4 lb. shrimp
2 - 3 firm tomatoes, diced
1 medium red onion, diced
1/3 C. cilantro
3 garlic cloves, minced
1 jalapeno, minced
2 tbsp clam juice
2 limes, juice
salt

12 tostadas

Directions

1. Get a large zip lock bag: Combine in it all the ingredients.
2. Seal it and place it in the fridge for 8 h.
3. Once the time is up, strain the ceviche then serve it.
4. Enjoy.

Ceviche Guyana

> Prep Time: 30 mins
> Total Time: 1 hr
>
> Servings per Recipe: 8
> Calories 959.2
> Fat 81.1g
> Cholesterol 129.6mg
> Sodium 205.4mg
> Carbohydrates 43.9g
> Protein 26.7g

Ingredients

- 1 lemon, halved
- 1 head garlic, halved
- 3 bay leaves
- 8 peppercorns
- sea salt
- 1 1/2 lbs. large shrimp, peeled
- 2 C. coconut milk
- 1/2 C. lime juice, plus more
- lime juice
- 1 red onion, sliced
- 2 serrano chilies, sliced
- 1/2 bunch cilantro leaf, chopped
- 4 coconuts split in half
- rock salt
- extra virgin olive oil

Directions

1. Bring a large saucepan of water to a boil. Stir in it the lemon, garlic, bay leaves, peppercorns, and salt.
2. Turn off the heat and stir in the shrimp. Let it sit for 4 min. Drain it, cool it down and slice it in half.
3. Get a mixing bowl: Stir in it the coconut milk, lime juice, onion, chilies, cilantro, and a pinch of salt.
4. Add the shrimp and toss them to coat. Place it in the fridge and let them sit for 35 min.
5. Remove the liquid from the coconut halves and reserve them for another use.
6. Pour some rock salt in a serving dish. Place in it the coconut halves and spoon into them the ceviches.
7. Serve them with extra toppings of your choice.
8. Enjoy.

HOW TO MAKE a Ceviche

Prep Time: 20 mins
Total Time: 20 mins

Servings per Recipe: 4
Calories 186.6
Fat 2.2g
Cholesterol 76.1mg
Sodium 132.1mg
Carbohydrates 19.7g
Protein 24.1g

Ingredients

1 lb. white fish fillet, cubed
3 - 4 limes, juice
1 red onion, sliced
1 large tomatoes, peeled, seeded, and chopped
green chili pepper, chopped
2 tbsp fresh coriander
1/4 C. corn
1 dash Tabasco sauce
1 tsp Worcestershire sauce
1 small lettuce, shredded
1 ear corn, cooked, cooled and cut into 4 pieces

Directions

1. Get a glass dish: Stir in it the fish with lime juice.
2. Cover it with a plastic wrap and let it sit for 8 to 9 h in the fridge.
3. Once the time is up, remove the fish from the juice and place it in a mixing bowl. Reserve the juice.
4. Stir the onion, tomato, chili, and coriander to the fish.
5. Get a mixing bowl: Whisk in it 2 tbsp of the reserved lime juice with oil, Tabasco and Worcestershire sauces.
6. Spoon the ceviche to serving glasses. Drizzle over them the lime dressing and serve them.
7. Enjoy.

Ceviche Polynesia

Prep Time: 35 mins
Total Time: 1 hr 35 mins

Servings per Recipe: 4
Calories   311.0
Fat   17.8g
Cholesterol   43.2mg
Sodium   637.4mg
Carbohydrates   11.5g
Protein   28.6g

Ingredients

- 1 lb. fresh ahi, cubed
- 1/2 quart lightly salt water
- salt
- 1 tsp salt
- 1 C. fresh lime juice
- 1 C. unsweetened coconut milk
- 1 tomatoes, chopped
- 1 small onion, chopped
- 1 red bell pepper, seeded and chopped
- 1 dash Tabasco sauce
- salt

Directions

1. Get a large bowl of water with a pinch of salt. Place in it the fish and let it sit for 35 min.
2. Once the time is up, drain it and transfer it to another bowl.
3. Pour over it the salt with lime juice. Toss them to coat and let them sit for 6 min.
4. Once the time is up, stir in the rest of the ingredients.
5. Chill the ceviche in the fridge for 35 min then serve it.
6. Enjoy.

ALASKAN
Ceviche

🥣 Prep Time: 25 mins
🕐 Total Time: 25 mins

Servings per Recipe: 8
Calories   296.8
Fat   18.7g
Cholesterol   52.3mg
Sodium   90.6mg
Carbohydrates   8.9g
Protein   24.2g

Ingredients

2 lbs. salmon fillets, skinned and cut into pieces
2 C. fresh lemon juice
2 medium tomatoes, seeded and diced
1 medium red onion, diced
1/2 C. olive oil
1/3 C. fresh lime juice
2 whole canned green chilies, rinsed and diced

1 tbsp cilantro, chopped
2 garlic cloves, minced
1/2 tsp cumin
1 dash hot pepper sauce

Directions

1. Get a mixing bowl: Stir in it the salmon with lemon juice.
2. Cover it with a plastic wrap and let it sit for 8 h in the fridge.
3. Once the time is up, remove the fish from the juice and transfer it to another bowl.
4. Add to it the rest of the ingredients and toss them to coat.
5. Refrigerate your ceviche in the fridge for about 30 min then serve it.
6. Enjoy.

Tacos Argentina

Prep Time: 10 mins
Total Time: 25 mins

Servings per Recipe: 6
Calories   138.5
Fat   5.1g
Cholesterol   115.2mg
Sodium   407.6mg
Carbohydrates   8.1g
Protein   16.5g

Ingredients

- 1/4 C. of lime juice
- 1 tbsp lime zest, grated
- 1 C. tomatoes, chopped & seeded
- 1 C. avocado, peeled & diced
- 1/2 C. cilantro, chopped
- 3/4 tsp salt
- 1/4 tsp pepper
- 3 garlic cloves, minced
- 1 lb. medium shrimp, peeled and cooked
- corn tortilla

Directions

1. Get a mixing bowl. Stir in it lime juice and zest.
2. Stir in the tomato, avocado, cilantro, salt, pepper, garlic, and shrimp. Cover the bowl with a plastic wrap.
3. Place it in the fridge and let it sit for 16 min while stirring it every 5 min.
4. Heat the tortillas in a pan or microwave. Place them on a board then spoon into them the ceviche.
5. Roll your tortillas then serve them it some sour cream.
6. Enjoy.

MARIA'S
Ceviche Platter

🥣 Prep Time: 15 mins
🕐 Total Time: 8 hr 15 mins

Servings per Recipe: 4
Calories   222.4
Fat   2.6g
Cholesterol   172.8mg
Sodium   535.8mg
Carbohydrates   25.2g
Protein   26.4g

Ingredients

1 lb. large shrimp, peeled and deveined
3/4 C. fresh orange juice
1/4 C. fresh lime juice
3 tbsp fresh lemon juice
2 large garlic cloves, minced
1 - 2 jalapeno, seeded and sliced
1/2 tsp dried oregano, crumbled
1/2 tsp ground pepper
1/2 tsp ground cumin

1 pinch ground cinnamon
1 pinch ground cloves
sea salt
hot sauce
1 medium red onion, sliced
1 medium tomatoes, seeded and diced
1/2 C. chopped cilantro
1 Belgian endive, spears separated, optional
1/2 C. ketchup

Directions

1. Get a mixing bowl: Mix in it the ketchup with the orange juice.
2. Stir in the lime and lemon juices, garlic, jalapeño, oregano, pepper, cumin, cinnamon, and cloves.
3. Stir in the hot sauce, shrimp, onion, tomato, cilantro, a pinch of salt and pepper. Toss them to coat.
4. Cover it with a plastic wrap and chill it in the fridge overnight.
5. Once the time is up, serve your ceviche with toppings of your choice.
6. Enjoy.

Pacific Island Ceviche

Prep Time: 15 mins
Total Time: 2 hr 45 mins

Servings per Recipe: 4
Calories	193.3
Fat	7.9g
Cholesterol	32.3mg
Sodium	60.4mg
Carbohydrates	10.1g
Protein	21.0g

Ingredients

- 12 oz. high grade tuna steaks, cubed
- 3/4 bunch green onion, sliced
- 1/4 small onion, diced
- 2 tsp grated ginger
- 1/4 C. lemon juice
- 1/4 tsp soy sauce
- 1/2 avocado, diced
- 1/2 mango, diced

Directions

1. Get a mixing bowl: Mix in it the onion, green onions, ginger, jalapeno, lemon juice, and soy sauce.
2. Stir in the tuna. Cover the bowl with a plastic wrap and chill it for 3 to 4 h in the fridge.
3. Once the time is up, adjust the seasoning of your ceviche then serve it.
4. Enjoy.

HOT
Plum Tomato Ceviche

Prep Time: 45 mins
Total Time: 45 mins

Servings per Recipe: 10
Calories 121.5
Fat 6.5g
Cholesterol 57.3mg
Sodium 270.8mg
Carbohydrates 10.0g
Protein 7.8g

Ingredients
1 lb. peeled and deveined medium shrimp
1 C. fresh lime juice
10 plum tomatoes, diced
1 large yellow onion, diced
1 jalapeno pepper, seeded and minced
2 avocados, diced
2 celery ribs, diced
chopped fresh cilantro
salt
pepper

Directions
1. Get a bowl: Stir in it the shrimp and pour over it the lime juice.
2. Cover it and let it sit for 12 min.
3. Get a serving bowl: Combine in it the tomatoes, onion, jalapenos, avocado, and celery.
4. Drain the shrimp and chop it. Add it to the veggies bowl with the strained lime juice.
5. Stir them to coat. Adjust the seasoning of your ceviche then serve it.
6. Enjoy.

California Ceviche Boats

🥣 Prep Time: 30 mins
🕐 Total Time: 1 hr 30 mins

Servings per Recipe: 6
Calories 341.6
Fat 24.3g
Cholesterol 43.8mg
Sodium 50.1mg
Carbohydrates 16.4g
Protein 18.6g

Ingredients

- 1 lb. trout, boned, skinned, and diced
- 1 C. lime juice
- 2 tbsp olive oil
- 1 medium onion, chopped
- 1 (4 oz.) cans green chilies, drained and chopped
- 1 medium tomatoes, peeled and chopped
- dried oregano
- salt
- pepper
- 3 ripe avocados, halved

Directions

1. Get a mixing bowl: Stir in it the fish with lime juice. Cover it with a plastic wrap and refrigerate it overnight.
2. Once the time is up, drain the fish and transfer it to a mixing bowl. Discard the juice.
3. Stir in the oil with onion, chilies, and tomatoes.
4. Scoop out some of the avocado flesh leaving the shell intact.
5. Dice the flesh add it to the fishbowl with a pinch of salt. Toss them to coat.
6. Spoon the ceviche to the avocado halves then serve them.
7. Enjoy.

ENJOY THE RECIPES?
KEEP ON COOKING WITH 6 MORE FREE COOKBOOKS!

Visit our website and simply enter your email address to join the club and receive your 6 cookbooks.

http://booksumo.com/magnet